"This is a remarkable resource for patients and their families as they struggle with the complexities of these disorders. Distilling clear-cut and direct recommendations from the current treatment literature, this book provides comprehensive information on how parents can facilitate their child's recovery."

—Douglas W. Bunnell, Ph.D.,
The Renfrew Center, Advancing the Education, Prevention, Research and Treatment of Eating Disorders

Helping Your Child Overcome an Eating Disorder

What You Can Do at Home

TECHNIQUES BASED ON THE
LATEST SCIENTIFIC RESEARCH
FROM EXPERTS AT THE YALE
CENTER FOR EATING AND
WEIGHT DISORDERS

BETHANY A. TEACHMAN, PH.D. • MARLENE B. SCHWARTZ, PH.D.,
BONNIE S. GORDIC, B.A. • BRENDA S. COYLE, PH.D.

Foreword by Kelly D. Brownell, Ph.D.

NEW HARBINGER PUBLICATIONS, INC.

Publisher's Note

This publication is designed to provide accurate and authoritative information in regard to the subject matter covered. It is sold with the understanding that the publisher is not engaged in rendering psychological, financial, legal, or other professional services. If expert assistance or counseling is needed, the services of a competent professional should be sought.

The Eating Attitudes Test (EAT-26) was reprinted with the permission of the Cambridge University Press.

Materials from the National Eating Disorders Association Web site were reprinted with permission from the National Eating Disorders Association. For more information: (800) 931-2237 or www.nationaleatingdisorders.org

Distributed in Canada by Raincoast Books

New Harbinger Publications, Inc.
5674 Shattuck Avenue
Oakland, CA 94609

Cover design by Poulson/Gluck Design
Edited by Brady Kahn
Text design by Michele Waters

ISBN-10 1-57224-310-4
ISBN-13 978-1-57224-310-1

Printed in the United States of America

New Harbinger Publications' website address: www.newharbinger.com

10   09   08

10   9   8   7   6   5   4   3   2

Contents

Foreword

On occasion a book comes along that can really help people. This is such a book. It does what's needed to be done: It provides an honest, helpful guide for families of people with an eating disorder.

Eating disorders can have a crippling, even deadly impact on the people who have them. Talented, impressive young people experience serious medical, psychological, and social problems. We can be thankful that eating disorders have been taken seriously by top scientists; hence, major advances have been made in treatment. This is good news indeed, but the puzzle still lacks certain pieces.

Families also suffer. Having a loved one with an eating disorder pushes one down a difficult path. There is concern coupled with a strong need to help. There is self-doubt. There are agonizing choices to be made every day. How should one talk about food? What should meals be like? What kind of help is needed? Who is expert enough to help? Who should be told? Is medication a good idea? When is a problem serious enough to require hospitalization? Should the person leave school or work to deal with the disorder? How can one tell when the problem is getting worse? What should families say? What should families do? Who is to blame?

One can find books, articles, and Web sites with advice on how families should deal with an eating disorder. The dilemma is knowing whom to trust. Authors have their own theories, often without supporting evidence. Some speak with great certainty and believe their approach applies to everyone. What emerges too often are baseball cap recommendations—one size fits all.

Such an approach does not square with the realities of eating disorders. People with eating problems have different symptoms and personalities, different needs and vulnerabilities. Families are not all the same. One size does not fit all families and is a poor fit for many. Professionals must help in ways best suited to a family's needs and styles. This book begins and ends with this philosophy.

The authors of this book have several important qualities. They understand the science of eating disorders and are alert to the most recent developments in the field. Being researchers themselves, they produce some of this new science. They are more than scientists, however. They are clinicians who work every day with real people and their families at the Yale Center for Eating and Weight Disorders. They are compassionate, intelligent, and insightful and wrote this book because they saw a very real human need.

This book is a blueprint to help families negotiate the tricky ground they face as their loved one gets help for an eating disorder. It helps bring structure to what feels like chaos. It helps families understand the disorder itself, what the loved one is experiencing, and how the person with the disorder, families, and health professionals can work together as a team. It can lift the blanket of hopelessness that can settle over families, not only because it provides specific guidance in areas where families really need help, but because the authors do this in a kind and compassionate way. Both the tone and the substance of this book reflect the expertise and caring of the authors.

This is a fine book by fine authors. Countless families will benefit.

—Kelly D. Brownell, Ph.D.
Professor of Psychology, Epidemiology and
Public Health
Director, Yale Center for Eating and
Weight Disorders
Yale University

Acknowledgments

We want to acknowledge all of the tremendous support and feedback we have received in preparing this book from our families, friends, and colleagues. We especially want to thank the members of the New Haven Eating Disorders Clinician Group and the clinical supervisors at the Yale Center for Eating and Weight Disorders for their careful reading and thoughtful comments on earlier drafts of this book. We would also like to thank Betty Litto for her very helpful administrative support. Most of all, we want to thank you and all of the families who struggle each day to help their children recover and live full and happy lives. We admire your courage and your strength, and we recognize the incredible challenges you are facing.

Above all, we want you to know that this resource is here to help *you*. We wish to give you a greater sense of how to facilitate your child's recovery. We hope to give you insight into the thoughts and feelings underlying your child's eating disorder and to provide you with the tools to better communicate with your child and other family members about their concerns.

Introduction

I heard the words the therapist said: "Your daughter has an eating disorder." But the meaning didn't really sink in. I thought only girls whose parents paid no attention to them got eating disorders. Besides, my daughter certainly doesn't look like those emaciated women you see on talk shows. How could this have happened in our family? Now what do we do?

> —Jane, parent of a sixteen-year-old girl with bulimia nervosa

You have just been told your child has an eating disorder. You go on the Internet look up "eating disorders" at an on-line bookstore, and find that there are over 700 books written on the topic. You begin to feel overwhelmed and confused. How can you get the straight answers you need?

This guide is designed to be an introductory resource to help you and your family learn what you can do when your child has been diagnosed with an eating disorder or if you suspect he or she has one. There is currently an overwhelming amount of information available, some of it scientifically sound and some of it not. Parents who are interested in understanding their child's eating problems and learning how to help are often in the difficult position of trying to distinguish between accurate information and unfounded theories and opinions. While we cannot answer all of your questions in this guide, we can help you sift through the overflow of available information. We will translate the latest scientific findings into understandable, useful guidelines for you and your child to use at home.

At the Yale Center for Eating and Weight Disorders, we regularly work with families in which a member has been diagnosed with anorexia nervosa, bulimia nervosa, binge eating disorder, or an eating disorder-NOS (not otherwise specified). We are committed to the scientific study of eating disorders and the importance of using treatments that have been evaluated and proven effective. At our clinic, parents often express confusion about the multitude of myths about why eating disorders develop and what is necessary to treat them. Meanwhile, adequate resources to help parents learn about eating disorders have not been readily available. This guide emerged as we began to put together resources for the families we treat at our clinic. As you try to find the answers that are right for your family, we hope this book will be like having your own eating disorders expert by your side.

We divided this book into seven chapters, each addressing a different aspect of eating disorders. Within each chapter, we debunk common myths about the topic, highlight the latest scientific research in the area, and respond to the questions we hear most frequently. In addition, we include descriptions of real clients and their families who have faced different challenges in their struggle with disordered eating. Each chapter includes interactive exercises so that you can apply what you have learned to your own family.

From the outset, we want to emphasize a few important points about how we view eating disorders and how we think families can best start to move forward:

Focus on support, not blame. Many people worry that if their child has an eating disorder it is because they have done something wrong as a parent. This is simply not the case. There is now strong evidence indicating that there are multiple causes of eating disorders, including environmental pressures, personality factors, genetic predisposition, and specific life events. The goal of this guide is not to judge or blame any particular member of the family. Rather, we want to think about how to promote those aspects of your family's functioning that encourage recovery and health. We hope to provide you with guidelines on how to address the issues within your family that may be hindering your relationship with your child and the treatment process. We recognize that having a child with an eating disorder can be both frightening and frustrating. Your family has already taken a significant step by looking for answers within this guide and perhaps entering the treatment process.

No two people are the same. While it is easy to speak of "eating disorders" in general, there are significant differences between anorexia nervosa, bulimia nervosa, and binge eating disorder. We will describe each of these three major eating disorders and help you understand how treatment goals vary depending on a person's specific symptoms. Bulimia nervosa is the most prevalent eating disorder among children and adolescents today, so much of the information in this guidebook will focus on this eating problem. We will also concentrate on anorexia nervosa and its symptoms, including restricted eating and weight preoccupation.

Just as different eating disorders require their own specific form of treatment and care, individuals with the same eating disorder diagnosis can be very different from one another. Each person will have her or his own unique experiences and needs. Therefore, you may find that some topics in this guidebook will be relevant to you and your child while others will not be relevant. You should not assume that your son or daughter is practicing all of the behaviors linked to disordered eating discussed in this guide. Instead, we recommend that you consider which scenarios are most relevant to your family and then, based on the advice provided here, decide how you want to handle your own situation.

Along the same lines, always keep in mind that the needs of your child are unique, based on his or her stage of development, personal history, and age. In this guide, we address a range of problems and offer many suggestions. We ask you to be aware of your child's unique set of strengths and limitations as you develop ideas about how to foster his or her recovery.

Family involvement is important. Since you are reading this guidebook, we already know that you are committed to helping your child. This is very significant because the younger the child, the more important it is to have the family involved in treatment. When a child is still living at home, we have found that it is critical to have the family involved in the treatment plan because of the important role that the family environment plays in the recovery process. When a child is away at college or has grown up and moved out on his or her own, it is sometimes logistically difficult but still beneficial to have the family included in treatment. Our belief is that families can play an important part in helping a family member get well. Recovery is usually best facilitated when families actively work together instead of against one another, so we encourage you to work with your child to support the treatment process. There are a variety of ways in which family involvement can be structured, and the treatment plan for your child and family can be developed based on your needs and availability.

Seek professional help. This guide is intended to help you learn about eating disorders and to support your child in his or her recovery. It is not a substitute for professional treatment. In the first chapter, we will discuss the signs and symptoms of eating disorders, and talk about how physically and psychologically serious eating disorders can be. If your child shows a number of the serious warning signs for an eating disorder, it is important to work with a professional who has specialized knowledge in this area. Although it can be difficult to talk about these issues with someone who is not part of your family, the consequences of eating disorders are too dangerous for you to carry the burden on your own.

Eating disorders are very serious, but recovery is possible. While it is easy to become discouraged when your child is ill and to feel like recovery is impossible, we firmly believe that one of the best things you can do for your child is to stay hopeful and supportive. At our clinic, we have seen severely ill young people, many of whom have been suffering with their eating disorder for years, go on to lead healthy, fulfilling lives. Full recovery is usually a long and challenging process, but it is our hope that you and your child will keep fighting to find a happier, healthier way of living and relating to food.

CHAPTER 1

What's Happening to Your Child?

Understanding and Evaluating Eating Disorders

When my son entered tenth grade he decided that he did not want to be the "fat kid" anymore. He began dieting and exercising, and at first, we were all proud of him. But then it seemed to get out of control and his weight continued to drop lower and lower. When I took him to the doctor, she said that he had anorexia nervosa. I couldn't believe it. How could this have happened to our son? Now what do we do?

—Elaine, mother of a seventeen-year-old
male with anorexia nervosa

There are few things more devastating for parents than to hear that their child is ill. Once the initial shock of the news wears off, you may be left with a range of feelings, from confusion and anxiety to guilt and anger. These are all normal reactions. It is likely that your feelings of distress are based in part on a lack of clear information about your child's condition and what can be done about it. You may be bewildered by the many myths and misconceptions about what eating disorders are and what happens to people who have them. The goal of this chapter is to help you make sense of your child's unhealthy behaviors, whether you suspect that your child has an eating disorder or if she or he has already received a diagnosis from a medical professional. Also, we hope to give you a sense of hope, because most people who seek treatment for eating disorders do get better.

The label "eating disorder" can actually refer to a wide range of behaviors and problems related to eating and weight. This chapter begins by helping to debunk some of the common myths about the nature of eating disorders. We include a quiz about eating disorders to help you test your knowledge. Next, we provide a list of warning signs to help you determine if your child is having difficulties with eating and weight. In addition, this chapter includes a detailed discussion of the different types of eating disorders and how to make sense of the diagnostic criteria that specialists use.

We will also discuss the possible medical and psychological problems associated with eating disorders and the rates of recovery and mortality. We want to emphasize the seriousness of eating disorders and to encourage you to have your child treated by a professional. The good news is that many people with eating disorders can recover fully, particularly if they have the support of their family. This chapter includes a section of frequently asked questions. It also includes some stories about other families and how they have coped as they learn about their child's eating problems for the first time. We will conclude, as we do every chapter, with a section called "Creating Solutions," to enable you to apply what you have been reading to your own family.

Debunking Myths about the Nature of Eating Disorders

Here are some commonly held myths, each followed by a discussion of the evidence that we know from research.

Myth: "Only really screwed up, crazy people get eating disorders."

Research says: Having an eating disorder does not mean that you are crazy. Many different kinds of people can develop eating problems, including people you know at work, school, or even in your own family and neighborhood. Taken together, anorexia nervosa and bulimia nervosa affect approximately 4 percent of young women in the United States today. Binge eating disorder is the most common eating disorder, affecting up to 4 percent of the general population (APA 1994).

Because eating disorders are so common, most of us come into contact with people who have them, whether we realize it or not. Although eating problems occur most frequently among young women, they can happen to people from all different backgrounds, ages, and socioeconomic groups.

Struggling with an eating disorder does not mean that a person is crazy or insane, but it does mean that they are in serious emotional and physical pain and in need of help.

Myth: "It's probably just a stage that kids go through."

Research says: Disordered eating is not an acceptable stage in any person's development. Although it is true that some people can get better from an eating disorder, most people need help so that their condition does not worsen and lead to even more severe psychological and physical consequences.

You should never assume that an eating disorder is just a stage that you do not need to worry about. Even if your child says that "everybody at school throws up after eating a lot," you should not presume that this is a normal behavior. The earlier a person seeks help, the better his or her chance for recovery (Fahy and Russell 1993). The symptoms of eating disorders are extremely harmful, so the sooner your family takes action, the better.

Myth: "My child doesn't look that skinny; she can't have an eating disorder."

Research says: People of all shapes and sizes can develop eating disorders. Actually, people who have bulimia nervosa (which is much more common than anorexia nervosa) are usually in the normal weight range. People with binge eating disorder often struggle with obesity. It is true that people with anorexia nervosa, the eating disorder most frequently portrayed in the media, are significantly underweight and often suffer terrible physical ramifications from being so extremely thin. Consequently, if your child is unusually thin, it could be an important warning sign. However, do not just assume that because a person is not underweight that he or she does not have an eating disorder.

Myth: "Eating disorders aren't real. Most people are just faking to get attention."

Research says: Eating disorders have *very* real psychological and physical consequences. People with eating disorders do not enjoy the problem and they do not feel good about themselves. Although it is true that eating disorders may continue in part because people get reinforced for their behavior (such as receiving special attention or compliments for losing weight), this is very different from the idea that the disorder is a sham.

Additionally, some people think that because anorexia and bulimia are mental health disorders, this means that these problems are not real, that they are just in the person's head, or that the person with an eating disorder is doing something on purpose. This is simply not true. Mental health disorders involve real problem behaviors that are painful and unhealthy. The person really believes that he or she needs to lose weight or avoid weight gain. While this belief may be difficult for you to understand and may seem irrational, it is certainly real enough to motivate a range of frightening and dangerous behaviors.

Getting the Facts

Almost everyone has heard of the term *eating disorders*, but many people do not know what it actually means. Some people think that eating disorders are only about food. Other people think that the problems are not real and that the person just wants attention. Still other people imagine that only young, Caucasian women in Western cultures can get eating disorders, or that eating problems are extremely rare conditions, or even that only exceptionally underweight people have eating disorders. Unfortunately, some people also think that eating disorders are useful because they lead to weight loss, and there's an assumption that people can have an eating disorder "just for a little while" to lose a few pounds. Learning the facts about eating disorders is an important part of figuring out how to get the help that your family needs.

Quiz: Test Your Knowledge

Take this quiz on common facts about eating disorders. The answers may astonish you.

1. Approximately what percentage of young women in the United States have anorexia nervosa, meaning that they are restricting their food intake to such a degree that they are starving themselves?

   a. 0.2 percent

   b. 1 percent

c. 5 percent

2. Around what percentage of college-aged women have bulimia nervosa, meaning that they regularly binge (eat a very large amount of food in a short period of time), and then engage in some kind of unhealthy behavior to compensate for the overeating (such as vomit, take laxatives, or overexercise)?

   a. .5 percent

   b. 1–2 percent

   c. 3–4 percent

3. What percentage of people who have had anorexia later go on to develop symptoms of bulimia?

   a. 5 percent

   b. 20 percent

   c. 50 percent

4. It is well known that the majority of people with anorexia are female, but what percentage of people with this disorder are male?

   a. 1–2 percent

   b. 10–20 percent

   c. 30–50 percent

5. What percentage of eleven-year-olds have already made one dieting attempt?

   a. 5 percent

   b. 10 percent

   c. 25 percent

6. According to a 1996 survey, approximately what percentage of women in the U.S. report that they are dissatisfied with their general appearance?

   a. 10–20 percent

   b. 20–40 percent

   c. 50–60 percent

7. What is the mortality rate for anorexia nervosa?

   a. 1–5 percent

   b. 6–10 percent

   c. 11–15 percent

8. In a survey of American children, what percentage of first-, second-, and third-grade girls report that they want to be thinner?

   a. 11 percent

   b. 42 percent

   c. 64 percent

9. What percentage of magazine fashion models appear to meet the weight criteria for anorexia nervosa?"

   a. 5 percent

   b. 10 percent

   c. 25 percent

10. People with bulimia nervosa tend to be:

   a. extremely underweight

   b. normal weight

   c. extremely overweight

11. What percentage of American women are currently trying to lose weight?

   a. 21 percent

   b. 30 percent

   c. 39 percent

12. What percentage of American men are trying to lose weight on any given day?

   a. 21 percent

   b. 30 percent

   c. 39 percent

13. Since binge eating disorder is a relatively new diagnosis, its prevalence in the general population is still being researched. However, it appears to affect males more than anorexia nervosa or bulimia nervosa. What is the approximate ratio of males to females with binge eating disorder?

   a. 1:3

   b. 1:2

   c. 1:1

14. The relationship between eating disorders and culture is complex. It seems that more Caucasian women in Western cultures develop eating disorders than do women of other backgrounds or geographic origin; however, people of all ethnicities can and

do develop eating problems. What factor makes it more likely that a female Mexican-American college student will develop eating-disordered symptoms?

    a. believing in U.S. societal views of attractiveness

    b. feeling dissatisfied with her body

    c. both of the above

15. Participation in which of the following sports is considered a risk factor for an eating disorder?

    a. lightweight rowing and wrestling

    b. distance running and figure skating

    c. all of the above

Answers to Quiz

1. b: Studies of women in late adolescence and early adulthood suggest prevalence rates of .4 to 1 percent for anorexia nervosa (American Psychiatric Association (APA) 1994).

2. c: College women are at the highest risk for bulimia nervosa with prevalence rates of 3 to 4 percent (Drewnowski, Yee, and Krahn 1988).

3. c: About half of patients with anorexia nervosa will meet the criteria for bulimia nervosa at some point in the course of their illness (Sullivan 2002).

4. b: In clinic samples, 10 to 20 percent of cases of anorexia nervosa are male (Andersen 2002).

5. c: By eleven years of age, up to one-fourth of girls will have made one dieting attempt; the average age of a girl's first diet is around twelve or thirteen (Hill 2002).

6. c: The 1996 survey found that 56 percent of women were dissatisfied with their overall appearance. This is more than double the rate of 23 percent found in 1972 (Cash 1997).

7. b: This substantial mortality rate is due to the physical consequences of starvation associated with anorexia nervosa and to suicide (Sullivan 2002).

8. b: In this study of over 1,000 children, girls chose a thinner ideal body shape for themselves, regardless of their age, weight, or race (Collins 1991).

9. c: A number of studies have shown that the "ideal" female body portrayed in the media has gotten thinner over the last several decades. Theorists believe that this may have contributed to the recent rise in eating disorders (Stice 2002).

10. b: Individuals with bulimia nervosa tend to be normal weight (Beaumont 2002). People assume that someone with an eating disorder must be visibly underweight; however, unhealthy eating can occur at any weight.

11. c: In our society, dieting has become so common that people consider it a normal behavior. This makes it harder to identify when someone has gone from simply dieting to developing an eating disorder (Hill 2002).

12. a: Although dieting is less common among men than women, many men are still dieting. Just like women, men need to learn how to make healthy dietary changes, and not fall into the fad diet trap (Hill 2002).

13. c: As the research on binge eating disorder has evolved, the most recent studies suggest that there are nearly as many males with binge eating disorder as females (Andersen 2002).

14. c: Women from ethnic minority groups can also develop eating disorders. It appears that they are at greater risk if they are dissatisfied with their bodies and endorse U.S. sociocultural values regarding attractiveness and thinness (Lester and Petrie 1995).

15. c: Sports that emphasize maintaining a low weight or require a lean body shape for performance are associated with higher rates of eating disorders than other types of sports (Byrne 2002).

Don't worry if you didn't get many answers right on the quiz. Most people don't score very high because there's little awareness of just how common and how serious eating disorders are. Hopefully you have learned something new from these statistics and realize that, although your child may be dealing with a difficult problem, you are certainly not alone.

Warning Signs

Many parents are confused about when it is appropriate for them to be concerned about their child's eating difficulties and when they may be overreacting. The truth is that without a formal evaluation there is no simple way to know. So, as a general policy, we recommend that you encourage your child to have an evaluation—again, the earlier you seek help, the better the chances for recovery.

The fact that you are reading this book suggests that your child has been diagnosed with an eating disorder or that you are concerned that your child might have one. The tricky part is that most young women show some signs of being dissatisfied with their body and wanting to lose weight. This unhappiness is called *normative discontent*, which is an unfortunate reality in a culture that idealizes thinness, stigmatizes obesity, and connects our self-worth to our physical appearance (Rodin, Silberstein, and Striegel-Moore 1984).

Sadly, many women in our society show some signs of disordered eating, which can take the form of poor body image, preoccupation with losing weight, and restriction of food intake. Many girls and women regularly take part in something called "fat talk," a phenomenon that involves speaking negatively about your body as a topic of conversation and a means of acceptance (Nichter 2000). However, this does not mean that all females who are dissatisfied with their bodies have an eating disorder, or that you should immediately rush your child to the hospital if you are suspicious. Instead, we encourage you to think about the risk for eating disorders as a combination of multiple factors, rather than associating it with one sign alone. It is essential to consider the severity of your child's behaviors relative to other people you know. Most importantly, you want to think about whether the thoughts, feelings, and behaviors related to eating problems are interfering in your child's life. The question of whether a person meets the technical criteria for a diagnosis is secondary to the question of whether or not these behaviors prevent the person from leading a healthy, full existence. Regardless of whether an individual can be classified as "anorexic" or "bulimic," professional help can be very beneficial if factors related to eating, shape, and weight are making it hard for him or her to feel good as a person and function well at home, school, work, or in relationships.

To help you catch the problem before it becomes worse, we have developed a checklist of common warning signs for anorexia and bulimia nervosa. The items on the checklist were drawn from self-report questionnaires as well as from clinical observation. Do your best to reflect on the many warning signs listed, but recognize that for many people eating disorders are kept very secret, so you simply may not know that these behaviors are occurring. Consequently, you shouldn't blame yourself for not knowing if your child is engaging in these behaviors.

The warning signs are divided into two categories based on their seriousness. Again, if you have any questions, we suggest that you seek a professional evaluation (a topic we will discuss in chapter 2).

Warning Signs Checklist

The warning signs are divided into sections and labeled as *possible signs* or *serious signs*.

- *Possible signs* are behaviors, thoughts, and feelings that suggest that your child *may* have an eating disorder or is at risk for developing an eating disorder. You are looking for a pattern where a number of risk factors seem to be present. Always consult a professional with any questions or concerns you may have about your child's health and possible eating disorder.

- *Serious signs* are behaviors, thoughts, and feelings that may pose more of a threat to your child's health and indicate that an eating disorder is likely. If you have checked off any of these items, we strongly recommend that you speak with a professional about your child's health and talk with your child about having an evaluation.

Place a check mark in the spaces provided if you know or suspect that your child is having difficulty with these behaviors, thoughts, and feelings:

Possible Signs

_____ Skips meals

_____ Takes very small portions (compared to others)

_____ Avoids eating in front of others/eats in secret

_____ Eats in a ritualistic way (e.g., chews each bite a certain number of times)

_____ Has very rigid rules about eating (e.g., won't eat past a certain time)

_____ Chews food but spits it out before swallowing

_____ Likes to shop and cook, but does not eat the meals he or she has prepared

_____ Regularly has excuses not to eat (e.g., not hungry, ate early, feels ill)

_____ Boasts about eating healthy food

_____ Becomes "vegetarian" but does not eat the necessary fats and oils

_____ Chooses primarily low-fat items to eat, with little balance

_____ Chooses primarily low-calorie items to eat

_____ Reads food labels all the time

_____ Always drinks diet sodas or chews gum

_____ Rearranges food on the plate to make it look like he or she is eating

_____ Feels "disgusted" by foods he or she used to like, especially high-fat items

_____ Categorizes food as "safe" or "good" versus "dangerous" or "bad"

_____ Thinks irrational thoughts about eating (e.g., "If I am thin, then I'll be happy"; "If I eat after 10 P.M., I'll gain twice the weight")

_____ Competes with others to eat the least and be the thinnest

_____ Becomes irrational or sulks when someone talks to him or her about eating

_____ Buys large amounts of a particular food, often a junk food

_____ Secretly takes food from cupboards or the refrigerator

_____ Leaves empty food packages lying around

_____ Wants to change shape and weight (more than regular "fat talk")

_____ Wears baggy clothes or layers to hide body shape or particularly disliked body parts

_____ Obsesses about his or her clothing size

_____ Spends lots of time inspecting self in the mirror

_____ Exercises to lose weight, rather than to promote health

Serious Signs

_____ Person binge eats (i.e., eats an unsually large amount of food at one time)

_____ Has dramatic weight loss (more than 5 percent of his or her normal weight, even though not ill)

_____ Is preoccupied with thoughts about food and weight, so that it is hard to concentrate on other things

_____ Denies hunger, even though he or she has not eaten for a long time

_____ Binges to escape stress and negative emotions, and avoids talking about feelings

_____ Goes to the bathroom immediately after eating, and you notice signs of vomiting (such as a dirty toilet, foul-smelling bathroom, running water or hairdryer to cover noise of vomiting, excessive use of mouthwash)

_____ Buys laxatives, diet pills, diuretics, or "natural" weight loss products

_____ Shows physical signs of vomiting, such as calluses on back of hands, unusual swelling of the cheeks or jaw, discoloration of teeth

_____ Has frantic fears of gaining weight or becoming obese

_____ Insists that you cannot feel good about yourself unless you are thin

_____ Exercises immediately after eating to avoid weight gain

_____ Exercises daily for more than an hour outside of scheduled team practices

_____ Consumes sport drinks and supplements, but not enough calories to support the athletic lifestyle

_____ Exercises even in bad weather, when ill, injured, or overtired

This checklist has been developed in part based on information discussed on the Web site of the National Eating Disorders Association (2001). In chapter 2, we will discuss other possible signs, such as social withdrawal, isolation, and moodiness. However, these problems are not exclusive to eating disorders (in other words, they can also occur for other reasons), so we did not include them in the checklist.

Definitions: Diagnostic Criteria for Eating Disorders

The criteria used by professionals to establish an eating disorder diagnosis is useful to help you think about how extreme or severe a behavior or symptom typically needs to be for it to be considered clinically significant. To be clinically significant, symptoms simply must be serious enough that they are causing distress and interfering with a person's everyday functioning. So, in this section, we outline each of the diagnostic criteria that are adapted from the *Diagnostic and Statistical Manual of Mental Disorders IV* (DSM-IV), which is the main resource used to diagnose eating disorders (APA 1994).

These criteria should not be thought of as absolute and rigid diagnostic guidelines; in fact, the criteria themselves can change as the manual is updated according to new research evidence. We encourage you to use this section as a way of familiarizing yourself with the terms and definitions you may hear when talking with medical and mental health professionals. We urge you to refrain from trying to diagnose your child. Keep in mind that it takes years of formal training to accurately diagnose an eating disorder, so please consult with or take your child to see a professional for a full evaluation if you are concerned.

Anorexia Nervosa

Anorexia nervosa is characterized by extreme weight loss and restrictive dieting. The individual is literally terrified of gaining weight even though he or she is noticeably underweight, and will often report feeling fat despite actually being very thin. Individuals frequently develop symptoms in early to mid-adolescence (during the onset of puberty at age twelve to thirteen) or during the transition to adulthood (age seventeen to eighteen). This disorder has one of the highest death rates of any mental health condition. There are four central diagnostic criteria for anorexia nervosa, which all need to be met for a person to receive this diagnosis. In addition to these criteria, other symptoms such as depression, irritability, withdrawing from friends and family, and strange eating habits often coincide with anorexia nervosa, but do not need to be present in order for an individual to receive a formal diagnosis. For example, the person may cut food up into tiny pieces before eating it, prepare gourmet meals for others to eat, and consider certain foods morally "good" or "bad."

Diagnostic Criteria: Anorexia Nervosa

- **Low weight.** The low weight criterion required for a diagnosis of anorexia is typically met when the individual's body weight is less than 85 percent of what is expected based on age and height. Lack of weight gain during childhood and puberty (when growth is anticipated) can also meet this criterion. Your child's doctor can help determine what the normal weight of your child should be and can then calculate to see if he or she has fallen too low. Note that it is possible for a person who binge eats and then purges to have anorexia if he or she is still seriously underweight.

- **Intense fear of gaining weight, even though at a very low weight.** This criterion reflects one of the psychological aspects of anorexia; the fear of weight gain is not based on any realistic evidence that a person has or will gain weight. In fact, people with anorexia frequently become more fearful of gaining weight or becoming fat as they progressively lose more weight.

- **Distorted image of shape or weight, overemphasis on shape or weight in evaluating him/herself, or denial of the consequences of the current low weight.** People with anorexia consistently believe that they are overweight and cannot see what they really look like in the mirror. Their preoccupation with losing weight takes over in such a way that it can distort their perception of their own body. They become unable to evaluate it objectively. At the same time, the obsession with being at a low weight becomes a central feature of how the person sees him or herself. Consequently, instead of placing value on how they treat others or how they are doing at school or in their relationships, their self-worth becomes dependent upon how thin they are and how extensively they can deny themselves food. While this is going on, the person may deny the seriousness of their weight loss, make excuses, or minimize the lengths they are going to in order to lose weight or avoid weight gain.

- **Amenorrhea: Not having a menstrual period for at least three consecutive months (in females who have already started to** menstruate). This can be a difficult criterion to evaluate especially if a woman is taking hormones, such as birth control pills, that may cause her to have her period despite her low body weight. In these cases, a person can still be diagnosed with anorexia, even if she is getting her period due to being on some kind of hormone supplement. Along this same line of thought, a child who is too young to menstruate would also not be evaluated on the criterion of amenorrhea. Similarly, in men, there is no obvious way to notice a comparable change in hormonal cycles. However, restrictive dieting and weight loss can in fact lead to a reduction in testosterone levels in men.

Bulimia Nervosa

Unlike anorexia nervosa, people struggling with bulimia nervosa often have an average body weight. Bulimia is characterized by a repeated cycle of binge eating, during which the person eats a large amount of food all at once and feels out of control while doing so, as though he or she cannot stop the binge. The binge is usually followed by some kind of compensatory behavior, such as vomiting, misuse of laxatives or diuretics, excessive exercise, or fasting, all of which can be used to get rid of the calories eaten during a binge. The rigid dieting between binges creates a cycle where the person becomes hungry and then binges again. As with anorexia, people with bulimia also often believe that their self-worth is tied to being thin, and as with anorexia, there are severe physical consequences to bulimia. There are five diagnostic criteria for bulimia nervosa (discussed below). Other symptoms that often accompany the disorder (but which are not required for a diagnosis) include feelings of depression, guilt, self-doubt, and anxiety. These feelings can occur even though the person appears to be competent and fun on the outside. He or she often has a secret life that may require complex schedules or rituals that provide opportunities for binge-and-purge sessions. The person generally recognizes that these behaviors are unhealthy, which adds to the shame and secrecy associated with the disorder. For some people, a number of impulsive behaviors, such as promiscuity, shoplifting, or abusing alcohol and drugs, can also be symptoms related to the disorder.

Diagnostic Criteria: Bulimia Nervosa

- **Reoccurring binge eating episodes.** These are described as 1) eating an unusually large amount of food in a given period of time, and 2) feeling a lack of control over what is eaten or how much is eaten. It is not always easy to judge what amount of food would constitute an "objective" binge (eating an unusually large amount of food). Consider what other people might eat under similar circumstances. Eating eight chocolate bars and a full box of cereal in one sitting would probably constitute a binge, but eating a giant portion of food at a holiday dinner would probably not constitute a binge.

Some people with bulimia feel that they have binged even when they eat a reasonable or small amount of food. This is called a "subjective" binge. For these people, normal eating episodes can feel just as scary and out of control as eating a large amount of food, and as a result, the person may feel just as compelled to do an unhealthy behavior (such as vomit or abuse laxatives) to compensate for the eating.

- **Reoccurring purging behaviors to prohibit weight gain.** This includes excessive exercise, vomiting, fasting, or abusing laxatives, diuretics, enemas, or other medications. According to one popular theory of eating disorders, the binge-purge cycle is a vicious circle in which a person tries to follow a rigid diet, which naturally leads to feelings of hunger and deprivation and subsequently causes the person to lose control and binge eat. The person then feels guilty for overeating and feels the need to compensate for the binge in an effort to prevent weight gain (Fairburn, Marcus, and Wilson 1993). These compensatory behaviors have serious psychological and physical health consequences and set the person up to continue the frightening binge-purge cycle.

- **Bingeing and purging behavior occur approximately twice a week for three months.** This criterion should only be used as a general guideline. If your child is bingeing and purging once a week only, or the behavior has only been going on for two months, do not assume that your child is okay and does not need help. Whether or not the frequency of the binge-purge cycle is sufficient to warrant a diagnosis should not disguise the central issue, which is whether this pattern is physically or emotionally unhealthy and is interfering with your child's well-being and functioning.

- **Overemphasis on shape or weight in evaluating him/herself.** As with anorexia nervosa, people with bulimia nervosa place an excessive amount of importance on their body shape and weight, and feel that they cannot be happy or worthwhile people if they are not thin. The preoccupation with weight and shape gets in the way of feeling fulfilled in other areas of their lives. For example, fasting can leave a person too tired to focus on schoolwork; excessive exercise can dominate a person's time, leaving few opportunities for other activities; and the secrecy of the binge-purge cycle can make it difficult to maintain a healthy social life and open, honest relationships.

- **These difficulties are not occurring during an episode of anorexia nervosa.** This final criterion is present to distinguish between individuals who have *anorexia nervosa binge-eating/purging type* from individuals with bulimia nervosa. Thus, a child who binges and purges but is not extremely low weight would receive a diagnosis of bulimia, whereas a child with severely low weight would receive the anorexia diagnosis. (People who are low weight and do not regularly binge eat or purge, but instead restrict their food intake to avoid weight gain, would be diagnosed as *anorexia nervosa restricting type*.) People with bulimia nervosa are often normal weight, despite the compensatory behaviors they engage in following the binge eating, because the purging behaviors and excessive exercise do not eliminate the majority of the calories the individual consumes during a binge.

Binge Eating Disorder (BED)

This disorder has recently been included as a research category in the *Diagnostic and Statistical Manual of Mental Disorders*, so it has been less researched than anorexia and bulimia nervosa. People with binge eating disorder (sometimes referred to as compulsive overeating) will frequently binge eat and feel out of control and unable to stop eating. During the binges, a person may eat rapidly and secretly, and feel ashamed and guilty afterwards. However, unlike people with bulimia who follow binges with compensatory behaviors, people with binge eating disorder do not regularly vomit, overexercise, or abuse laxatives or diuretics. The five diagnostic criteria for binge eating disorder are listed below. You will notice some overlap with the criteria for bulimia, given that both disorders are characterized by binge eating.

Diagnostic Criteria: Binge Eating Disorder

- Reoccurring binge eating episodes, which are described as both:
    1. eating an unusually large amount of food in a given period of time, and
    2. feeling a lack of control over what is eaten or how much is eaten

- Episodes of binge eating include three (or more) of the following:
    1. eating much faster than usual
    2. eating while feeling full and uncomfortable
    3. eating large quantities of food even though not hungry
    4. eating alone and feeling ashamed by the amount of food being eaten
    5. having feelings of disgust, depression, or guilt after overeating

- Experiencing distress due to binge eating.

- Binge eating episodes occur approximately two days a week for six months.

- There is no regular use of purging behaviors, and binge eating is not occurring during episodes of anorexia or bulimia.

It is estimated that up to 4 percent of the population suffer from binge eating disorder (APA 1994). While not all people with this disorder are overweight, research suggests that approximately 8 percent of the people who are obese also have binge eating disorder (Grilo 2002). Unlike anorexia or bulimia, this disorder is split fairly equally among the sexes. Individuals with binge eating disorder tend to feel worse about their bodies and have more struggles with depression and anxiety than other overweight people who do not engage in binge eating. People may binge eat as a result of trying to stick to an overly rigid diet or because of emotional reasons. For example, some people binge eat to comfort themselves after stressful events or to numb emotional pain.

Eating Disorder–Not Otherwise Specified (ED-NOS)

ED-NOS stands for eating disorders-not otherwise specified and is essentially a grab bag to refer to all different types of people who have symptoms of an eating disorder but do not meet all the criteria for a specific diagnosis. For example, women who are low weight, fear weight gain, and are preoccupied with their shape but continue to get their period would be diagnosed with ED-NOS, rather than anorexia (because they do not meet the amenorrhea criterion). Similarly, a person who binges three times in one week and vomits after each episode but then does not binge at all for the next two weeks would be diagnosed with ED-NOS, rather than bulimia. By no means should you think that a diagnosis of ED-NOS means that it is "not a real eating disorder" or is not serious. In fact, many people who are referred to clinics for treatment will receive an ED-NOS diagnosis for one reason or another, given the high degree of specificity in the anorexia and bulimia criteria. The important question is whether the person's eating disorder symptoms are interfering in his or her life and causing distress.

How Serious Are Eating Disorders?

Talking to families about the seriousness of eating disorders is always difficult. Some of the symptoms of eating disorders (such as being dissatisfied with body shape or wanting to lose weight) are very common behaviors and do not necessarily represent a severe health risk. Just because you have noticed that your child refused an ice cream cone one day does not mean that he or she has an eating disorder and that you should become excessively concerned. However, eating disorders can be life-threatening and their seriousness is very real. It is important that you arm yourself with the facts about the dangerousness of eating disorders so that you and your family can take action quickly if it is required.

Medical Complications

The following information about the medical and psychological consequences of eating disorders was adapted from the Web site of the National Eating Disorders Association, a non-profit organization. We have included lists of specific medical and psychological complications, and these lists were reprinted with permission from the National Eating Disorders Association (2001).

Remember that this is a list of potential complications, so not every person who has one of the eating disorder diagnoses will suffer these physical consequences. However, the risks are serious, so always consult with a medical professional if you are concerned about your child's health. It is always better to catch a problem earlier, rather than to wait for it to get worse.

Health Consequences of Anorexia Nervosa

The primary medical problems associated with anorexia nervosa result from self-starvation, which causes the body to slow down all of its normal processes in an attempt to conserve energy. By denying one's body the nutrients it needs, a person becomes vulnerable to a number of serious health consequences such as:

- Abnormally slow heart rate and low blood pressure, leading to increased risk for heart failure

- Reduction of bone density (osteoporosis), which results in dry, brittle bones

- Muscle loss and weakness

- Severe dehydration, which can result in kidney failure

- Fainting, fatigue, and overall weakness

- Dry hair and skin, and hair loss

- Growth of a downy layer of hair called "lanugo" all over the body, including the face, in an effort to keep the body warm

Health Consequences of Bulimia Nervosa

The medical complications resulting from bulimia nervosa are due mainly to the recurrent binge-and-purge cycles. The compensatory behaviors associated with bulimia can affect the entire digestive system, and lead to electrolyte and chemical imbalances in the body. Electrolytes simply refer to substances in a solution that conduct electricity and are necessary for your body's health and functioning. In the body, an electrolyte imbalance results from dehydration and loss of potassium and sodium, which occurs following purging behaviors. These imbalances, in turn, can damage the heart and other major organ functions. Potential health consequences of bulimia nervosa include, but are not limited to:

- Electrolyte imbalances, leading to irregular heartbeats and possible heart failure and death

- Potential for gastric rupture during periods of binge eating

- Inflammation and possible rupture of the esophagus from frequent vomiting

- Tooth decay and staining from stomach acids released during frequent vomiting

- Chronic irregular bowel movements and constipation as a result of laxative abuse

- Peptic ulcers and pancreatitis

Health Consequences of Binge Eating Disorder

The majority of the medical risks associated with binge eating disorder are due to the health impacts of clinical obesity, including:

- High blood pressure

- High cholesterol levels

- Heart disease as a result of elevated triglyceride levels

- Secondary diabetes

- Gallbladder disease

Psychological Problems

Remember that eating disorders are a mental health problem, not just a threat to physical health and well-being. The following list of psychological problems, though not exhaustive, covers many of the critical areas potentially related to an eating disorder.

One thing to keep in mind as you read this list is that we do not always know which problem comes first. In some cases, it may be that a person is depressed and subsequently develops an eating disorder, but in other cases, a person can have the eating problem first and then become depressed as a consequence. So, you should think of this as a list of problems that can potentially accompany an eating disorder, rather than one problem necessarily causing the other.

- Depression (sometimes severe enough to lead to suicide)

- Feeling of being out of control and helpless to do anything about personal problems

- Anxiety, self-doubt

- Guilt and shame

- Suspicion of others wanting to interfere, may include slight paranoia

- Fear of discovery

- Obsessive thoughts and preoccupations

- Compulsive behaviors; rituals dictating most activities, especially around food

- Feelings of alienation and loneliness

- Feelings of hopelessness

We recognize that it has probably been frightening to read this information about the potential medical and psychological complications associated with eating disorders. Our aim is to inform you of just how serious eating disorders can be. There is a lot of great help available, so if you think your child has an eating disorder, your job now is to encourage him or her to seek treatment as soon as possible and to stick with it. Remember that most people make a full recovery, so do not give up hope.

Recovery Rates

While the treatment of eating disorders is still a relatively new field, the techniques are continuing to get better and better, meaning that more people can achieve a full recovery. It is difficult to know exactly what percentage of people recover, and to what extent, because some treatments are more effective than others and some groups of people respond more easily to treatment than others (see chapter 6 regarding what you can expect in therapy). For example, the treatments for bulimia tend to be more effective and work faster than those for anorexia. Regardless of the disorder, however, the encouraging recovery rates make the value of treatment obvious.

Recovery from Bulimia Nervosa

Based on a review of many studies evaluating recovery rates from bulimia (Keel and Mitchell 1997), it is estimated that:

- 50 percent of people with bulimia fully recover

- 30 percent partially recover

- 20 percent show no recovery and report poor treatment outcomes

Recovery from Anorexia Nervosa

A recent study evaluating the recovery rates for women with anorexia (Fichter and Quadflieg, 1999) found that:

- 35 percent fully recovered

- 38 percent partially recovered

- 21 percent showed poor recovery

- 6 percent died

Recovery from Binge Eating Disorder

Studies show that:

- 60 percent fully recovered after one year of treatment (Wilfley 2002).

- Antidepressants reduced binge eating by 60 to 90 percent (Devlin 2002).

The most important message to draw from these statistics is that recovery is possible! It is usually a bumpy road that requires a lot of steps forward and backward before healing is achieved. At different stages of their lives, people may be more or less willing and capable of doing the hard work it takes to recover their mental and physical health, so do not assume that because a person has not succeeded in one treatment that this means he or she never will succeed. The costs of having an eating disorder are enormous, so try to stay hopeful and supportive of your child's efforts to recover; you may be surprised at how much a person's life can ultimately change and improve.

Questions and Answers about the Nature of Eating Disorders

Question: "My daughter doesn't take this seriously and doesn't want to consider getting help. What can I do?"

Answer: Unfortunately, it is common for young people to minimize the seriousness of their eating disorder. One reason for this may simply be a lack of understanding of the medical and psychological consequences of eating disorders and the mistaken belief that "extreme dieting is something everyone does" or that "you can just have an eating disorder for a little while until you lose weight." Others may minimize the seriousness of the problem because they do not want to give up the eating disorder. Although your daughter probably does not like the symptoms of fatigue, hunger, and secrecy that accompany an eating disorder, she probably does like the symptom of weight loss. When a person likes some of the symptoms of an illness, we call this *egosyntonic*. In contrast, when a person dislikes the symptoms (which is the case with most illnesses), we call this egodystonic. The fact that people like some of the eating disorder symptoms makes it especially hard to motivate them to change.

Let your daughter know that you are worried about her and that eating disorders are serious and very dangerous. You can talk with her and provide her with information to read about eating disorders (see the Resources section at the end of the book). Do not be disheartened if she is not immediately responsive to your efforts to get her professional help. Keep trying! Sometimes it takes a while to help a person see that she is suffering from the eating disorder because weight loss may be seen as such a positive outcome. If your daughter is under eighteen, you may decide that the condition is serious enough to warrant requiring her to go to treatment even if she is not initially willing. If she is an older teenager, you may not be able to exert this level of influence. In this case, your role is to be available to your child and to help her access resources as soon as she is willing. Make sure she understands how concerned you are and that you want to aid her in finding the help she needs. Beyond these steps, you cannot ultimately hold yourself responsible for her choice to enter or remain in therapy. So, even though this situation is very frustrating and worrisome, do not give up and do not blame yourself for your child's choices.

Question: "I feel like I've lost my child—she's rude to me now, mopes around all the time, and I know she's taking money from my purse. Who is this stranger in my house?!"

Answer: This is a very tough issue because it is not unusual for parents to explain that, while they still love their child, it is hard to like their child's behavior right now. This is a natural reaction to the behaviors your child is exhibiting. We encourage you to try to separate the symptoms of the eating disorder (including the moodiness and taking money) from the person that your daughter is. When a person has an eating disorder, he or she will do all kinds of things that normally would have seemed unthinkable. We are not suggesting that you let these behaviors slide, only that you try to understand where they come from and view them as part of the eating disorder your daughter is struggling with, instead of as part of the person your daughter is. Nonetheless, behaviors such as rudeness and stealing are simply not acceptable and should be dealt with appropriately.

Latisha's Story

Latisha had always been a chubby child. In the fall of her senior year, she told her mother, Carol, that she wanted to lose weight before going to college. Her mother thought she could lose a few pounds herself, so they decided to join Weight Watchers together. Latisha was a model group member and followed the diet perfectly. Her mother tried to help her by buying the right foods and not buying sweets and high fat desserts. At first it seemed like everything was going well. Latisha and Carol both lost about ten pounds and they were happy. Carol began playing tennis and going to a gym, and Latisha began running each morning.

Around February of her senior year, however, Latisha's weight loss seemed to be spiraling out of control, and she was starting to look too thin. She had lost almost thirty pounds, and Carol told her that she had lost enough weight and needed to start eating normally again. Latisha argued with her and said that if she started eating the way she used to, she would just get fat again. Carol was baffled; she felt like she was giving her daughter mixed messages. She felt guilty for having taken her to Weight Watchers in the first place, but she had never imagined that this could happen.

Latisha's friends began calling Carol and saying that they were worried. They said Latisha never ate lunch at school and always told them that she'd had a big breakfast that morning. They said she denied having an eating disorder and responded to their concern by saying that they were just jealous because they wanted to be thin enough to wear a size 0. Carol decided to call an eating disorders clinic to get some help. Although she feared that Latisha would be mad at her, Carol was more afraid that her daughter's health was in jeopardy.

The therapist explained that the first step of treatment involves an evaluation. She asked to meet with Latisha first and then to meet with

Latisha along with her parents at the end of the initial session. Carol made an appointment and then told Latisha the news. Latisha was furious. She told her mother to forget it, and she refused to go. She said that no one was going to make her do anything she didn't want to do and that she certainly didn't want to talk to some stranger. She insisted that her weight loss was not a problem. It was hard for Carol to see Latisha so upset. Even though she wanted to stop her daughter from crying and arguing, however, Carol continued to hold firm with her belief that an evaluation was necessary. She explained that the evaluation would provide information about whether or not Latisha had an eating disorder. And she refused to argue with her daughter. Carol stayed calm, which was especially difficult with Latisha yelling at her. But she managed to be insistent without being loud or argumentative, and eventually Latisha agreed to meet with the therapist.

During the evaluation, the therapist asked many questions about many parts of Latisha's life, not just about her eating and weight. Latisha found that she liked talking about her thoughts and feelings, her family and friends, and her classes and interests. Even though she continued to insist that her weight was not a problem, Latisha agreed to continue meeting with the therapist to learn more about herself. When she and her parents met together with the therapist, they all agreed on a treatment plan, which included a medical exam to assess Latisha's physical health, a consultation with a nutritionist, weekly individual therapy, and monthly family meetings. Although Latisha hadn't fully agreed that her eating and weight were serious issues, she liked the therapist and wanted to talk with someone outside of her family about things that bothered her. Her parents were relieved that professionals would be monitoring their daughter.

Kenny's Story

Kenny was sixteen years old and a star soccer player when his parents began to worry about his eating. As a child, Kenny had always been taller and heavier than his peers. Kenny was very muscular, and at five feet ten inches, he weighed 190 pounds. His parents noticed that he was gaining weight. In addition, they noticed that certain foods, such as ice cream and cookies, were disappearing from the kitchen as soon as they were purchased. Once, Kenny's mother thought she even noticed the bathroom smelling of vomit after Kenny had been in there. Kenny's parents confronted him and asked him if he was having difficulty with his eating. Kenny said that he was and he didn't know what to do. He told them that he had been trying to lose weight, but he also felt really hungry much of the time.

Kenny had been a soccer player since he was five years old. In fact, he and his parents both hoped that his soccer skills might help him get into a good college. Kenny spent two hours at soccer practice every day after school. His coach had mentioned to him that he thought he might be able to run faster if he lost a few pounds, so Kenny had been trying to restrict his food. But he found that he was starving at night after practice and ended up getting up in the middle of the night and eating sweets. He even tried throwing up once after binge eating.

Kenny and his parents went to have an evaluation with a therapist who felt that Kenny was binge eating as a result of trying to restrict his food intake while remaining very physically active. Kenny began treatment and learned that he needed to eat enough to fuel his body during the day in order to avoid binge eating at night. Kenny's pediatrician confirmed that his health was excellent and his weight was normal for an athlete with his build. The therapist explained to Kenny and his parents that Kenny was at the right weight, and given his excellent health status, he certainly should not try to lose any weight. Kenny and his parents felt that he would be happier if he lost a few pounds, as he had always been self-conscious about his size. The therapist explained that Kenny could develop his self-confidence and social skills, regardless of his weight. Going on a restrictive diet to make his body into something it was not would perpetuate the eating disorder. Kenny and his family agreed that his health was more important than anything. They all worked to have healthy foods available at home and to make sure that Kenny ate enough to support his athletic endeavors.

Creating Solutions

In this chapter we have reviewed a lot of information about the prevalence, signs, and symptoms of eating disorders. Now it may be useful for your family to discuss what has occurred in your own situation and to identify ways to talk with your child about your concerns.

Identifying Problem Areas

Here are some questions to ask yourself before you open the discussion with your child. Fill in the blanks.

What changes have you observed in your child's eating and exercise behavior?

_____

_____

_____

When did you start to notice these changes?

_____

_____

_____

Which of these changes worry you?

_____

_____

_____

Once you have identified the behaviors that worry you, the next step is to sit down with your child and discuss them. Clearly, this is easier said than done! It is quite common for people with eating disorders to feel protective of the disorder because they want to keep trying to lose weight and do not want to acknowledge that they are doing anything dangerous. Inside their heads is a voice telling them that they have found a good solution to their problems; they can feel in control, successful, and relieved when they engage in the behaviors of purging or not eating.

You know your child best. Therefore, we suggest that you (and/or other important adults in your child's life) sit down with your child and present these ideas in the way you believe he or she can best hear them. Here are some messages we think are important to convey:

- "We love you very much. That is why we want to talk about our worries about your health."

- "We've noticed some changes in your behavior. Specifically, we've noticed you are . . ." You might add, "eating less," "losing weight," "going to the bathroom immediately after meals," or "skipping dinner."

- "We are worried about this because we know your behaviors are signs of eating disorders."

- "Even though you may not believe you have an eating disorder, we also know that eating disorders can be very tricky and subtle."

- "Because we love you and feel responsible for helping you stay healthy, we want to arrange for a professional evaluation to see if you have an eating disorder and figure out what we can all do to help the situation."

Talking to Your Child about Your Concerns

Come up with some of your own statements to express your concerns to your child:

- _____

_____

_____

- _____

_____

_____

Our experience is that it takes most parents a few tries before they are able to get their child's consent to go for help. One strategy that you may try is to have a discussion about the pros and cons of having an evaluation. As a family, you can brainstorm the benefits and costs of pursuing help. This provides a way for your child's concerns to be heard and acknowledged, as well as a way for you to offer your views on why this may be a worthwhile endeavor. If you create a list of pros and cons, you may be able to show that the positives outweigh the negatives.

Pros and Cons of an Evaluation

Pros   **Cons**

_____   _____

_____   _____

_____   _____

_____   _____

_____   _____

_____   _____

In the meantime, remember that you and the rest of the family are under a lot of stress when living with someone whose health may be in jeopardy. You will be best able to help your child if you are feeling well yourself. Think about things you can do to make life easier for all of you at home. Perhaps you and your significant other need to take time to spend alone together to reconnect. Other children in the family may need for you to spend time attending to their concerns. If there are things you can do to reduce your own level of stress, you will be better able to fill your role as a parent. Take a few moments to brainstorm ideas of things that would help you out.

Taking Care of Yourself

Create a list of regular activities you can enjoy with your spouse or other significant adults, and remember to note _when_ you can do these.

Activity   **Day of the Week
                                                   and Time**

_____   _____

_____   _____

_____   _____

_____   _____

_____   _____

_____   _____

Create a list of activities for you and your children to do together, and schedule these into your busy week.

Activity   **Day of the Week and Time**

_____   _____

_____   _____

_____   _____

_____   _____

_____   _____

_____   _____

Create a list of activities for you to do alone, and always remember the importance of taking time for yourself.

Activity   **Day of the Week and Time**

_____   _____

_____   _____

_____   _____

_____   _____

_____   _____

_____   _____

Remember that your needs and concerns are important too. Finding ways to decrease your stress and enjoy yourself and others can be especially important during difficult times. Also keep in mind that expressing your concerns can be helpful. Sometimes parents feel that if they tell their child they are worried about his or her eating behavior, they may inadvertently cause things to get worse rather than better. There is no research evidence to support this view. Don't be afraid to express your love and concern.

Assessing Eating Problems

Without a formal evaluation, there is no way to know whether or not your child has an eating disorder, but questionnaires, such as the one provided in appendix A, can provide more information about your child's eating problems. Asking your child to complete the EAT can serve as a step toward acknowledging his or her eating problems and opening lines of communication. The results, for example, can indicate the severity of problems and point out particular areas causing distress. This information can be used to identify which symptoms are most significant and can help to determine the kind of help you need.

The Eating Attitudes Test (EAT) in appendix A was developed by Garner and colleagues (Garner, et al. 1982) and is one of the most frequently used tests for identifying problems associated with eating disorders. Instruments such as the EAT should be used only as a way to screen for eating problems and should never be used to diagnose an eating disorder. It is especially important that you, as a parent, not attempt to take on the responsibility of diagnosing your child. Your job is to be supportive by doing things such as listening to your child's concerns and encouraging your child to be curious about his or her thoughts, feelings, and behaviors. Acting as an expert about eating disorders will probably not serve either of you well.

When discussing these issues with your child, try to listen attentively without expressing criticism or judgment. Your child probably has strong feelings about this and may feel ashamed already, so your way of responding will mean a lot. Even if you do find yourself surprised by the severity of the problems, try to be accepting of your child's feelings. Do what you can to allow your child to feel comfortable opening up to you. Remember that there is a lot of great help available for people with eating disorders. By simply completing the questionnaire, your child is taking a step toward confronting his or her eating problems, which demonstrates reason for hope.

If your child is not ready to complete the questionnaire right away, encourage him or her to consider it and state that you are available to talk at any time.

CHAPTER 2

What Should You Do Now?
Finding a Therapist and Making Changes at Home

Yesterday, the principal at my daughter's school called. She said that my husband and I should come down as soon as we could to meet with our daughter and one of her teachers. When we got there, we learned that our daughter had been throwing up for weeks and had told one of her teachers. Now that we know, how can we address it right away at home? And how can we find a therapist to help her?

—Katherine, mother of a seventeen-year-old girl with bulimia nervosa

At this point, we assume that you have determined that your child's eating problems have become serious enough to require a professional evaluation and treatment. This can be a scary time because you want to find the right therapist for everyone involved, yet you may not know where to begin. You may have other concerns as well. Some families have difficulty letting others in on their personal business; it may feel inappropriate or even dangerous. Other families have a hard time allowing their child to see a therapist because it feels like a sign of failure in parenting. While these thoughts and emotions are natural and understandable, it is important to realize that eating disorders are a type of illness. There should be no more shame in seeking treatment from a professional for an eating disorder than there is in seeing a doctor for a broken arm. In fact, seeking the appropriate help for your child is a sign of good parenting.

You are taking an important step just by reading this chapter. First we will debunk some of the myths you may have heard about dealing with eating disorders. Then we will provide you with some information about different professionals who treat eating disorders, some guidance in finding the right therapist, and some strategies to help you handle things at home to facilitate your child's recovery. There is a lot that you can do! In addition to addressing some of the common questions we hear from concerned parents and giving some case examples of young people struggling with the same issues as your child, we also want to help you create solutions for your family. Along these lines, the chapter concludes with some strategies for finding the right therapist for your family and making changes at home.

Debunking Myths about Recovery

Myth: "No one with an eating disorder ever recovers. They are messed up for life."

Research says: Treatment for eating disorders can help. Your child can recover and stay well. It is impossible to provide a guarantee to any given family that therapy will work for their child, but research does indicate that specialized treatments for eating disorders can be highly effective for the majority of people who seek therapy and stick with it. In fact, approximately 80 percent of individuals suffering from bulimia nervosa and 73 percent with anorexia nervosa experience full or partial recovery (Fichter and Quadflieg 1999; Keel and Mitchell 1997). So, you should not give up hope!

If your child does not recover quickly, this does not mean that he or she will not succeed in treatment at another time. Some kinds of treatment work better for some people than for others, so your child may need to try more than one form of therapy. In addition, motivation varies. This is especially true of a young person who is sick. At various life phases and different stages of the disorder, your child may be more or less able to engage in the hard work of therapy. The bottom line is that people do get better from eating disorders, so do not become pessimistic.

Myth: "People with eating disorders end up being locked away in hospitals."

Research says: Hospitalization only occurs when the problem has become extremely severe and is needed to prevent suicide or a medical crisis. There are many alternative treatments that can be tried first. Rather than hospitalization, most eating disorder treatments initially involve individual or group therapy. Depending on the severity of your child's illness and the therapist's style, the sessions will probably occur at least once a week.

During therapy, children are usually still able to live at home and continue with many of the normal aspects of their lives. The purpose of treatment is not to stop your child's life (or your family's functioning), but to restore it. In addition to psychotherapy, your child may simultaneously see a psychiatrist, or another person who prescribes medication; a nutritionist to help establish normal, healthy eating; a physician to assess and monitor medical complications; and sometimes a dentist to repair damage caused by purging. Parents may also become involved in family counseling or a support group.

Hospitalization is necessary only in crisis situations, but it is important that you listen to specialists' advice if they say that it is needed for your child. The consequences of not hospitalizing someone who is dangerously low weight or might hurt him- or herself are serious. You should not assume hospitalization will be required, but you should also listen very seriously if it is recommended.

Myth: "It doesn't matter what I say or do. It shouldn't matter if I'm on a diet or am concerned about my shape and weight. Kids don't listen to their parents anyway."

Research says: Actually, parents can play a powerful role in helping to prevent eating disorders in their children and in helping to promote recovery. It is important that you be aware of the examples that you set for your son or daughter in your daily lifestyle. Focusing excessively on your own shape or weight, going on fad and extreme diets, or overemphasizing the importance of appearance may send the wrong messages about food and eating to your child. Not doing so can be a challenge because we live in a society that is preoccupied with weight and shape, and most American women have dieted at some point in their lives. Some studies have found that mothers of children with eating disorders often have a history of dieting themselves and display a greater preoccupation with body shape and weight than do mothers of children who do not suffer from eating problems (Pike and Rodin 1991). In this way, your behavior toward food and exercise, be it positive or negative, can greatly influence your child's risk in the development of eating difficulties.

Even though you may feel like you have little control over the progression of your child's eating disorder, the support you provide will be an important part of your child's recovery. Keep in mind that adolescents are often not able to say that they need you or to thank you for the efforts you make, but this does not mean that your role as a supportive parent is not appreciated and incredibly helpful.

How to Find a Therapist

Now that you have read chapter 1 and thought about the seriousness of your child's eating problems, it is time to seek professional help. It may be that your child simply needs an evaluation, or your child may need more serious intervention. This step can seem like a daunting task, but a number of ideas can help you get started. First you need to figure out where to look to find an eating disorder specialist near you. Next, you need to find the right therapist for your family. This may be your first time seeking help for a mental health problem, and you may not know what issues to consider.

Getting help for your child can be a confusing emotional step and can generate many concerns. Let us first consider some of the common issues people seeking professional help encounter.

Getting the Most Out of Treatment

Mental health treatment is a service industry, which means that you are a paying consumer who can request appropriate services for your child or family. This is the case even if your insurance company is actually paying the bills. Appropriate service does not mean that you can request or expect assurance that your child will fully recover in a specified time. Therapists cannot make promises about the outcome of any treatment for a specific person, just as a physician cannot promise that a certain medicine will cure an illness. However, therapists can and should explain to you what treatment consists of and why they chose this approach for your child.

We encourage you to feel confident in your rights as a consumer. Look around for the right person for your family. Make sure that the therapist has the specialized knowledge and skills your child needs, and do not hesitate to ask questions about what you can expect in treatment. Of course, it is important to keep in mind that the first time you meet the therapist, it will feel somewhat awkward. Try not to make premature judgments. Ask the questions that are necessary for you to feel comfortable.

Is a Specialist Really Necessary?

Often people feel confused about whether they want an eating disorder specialist or a clinician who can provide general support about life and relationship issues. This can be especially true in cases where the child is reticent to acknowledge his or her eating problems and may feel more open to talking about issues other than eating. The problem is this allows the child to continue to believe the eating is not a serious problem. While clinicians and counselors who provide "supportive psychotherapy" can be valuable (and you may consider seeing someone like this to help you during this time), we recommend that you find a specialist to help specifically with the treatment of the eating disorder for your child. The research tells us that recovery from eating disorders is more likely to occur with a specialist than with a general counselor. In fact, mortality rates are lower for people with anorexia nervosa who receive specialized and comprehensive medical and psychotherapeutic treatments (Crisp, et al. 1992).

Taking Advantage of a Team Approach

Treatment of eating disorders often requires a team approach because eating disorders often have both significant mental and physical complications that need to be monitored. Additionally, people who are young or who have been struggling with an eating problem for an extended period of time may not actually know what constitutes a normal, healthy diet. They may require treatment and monitoring by a dietician or nutritionist. Many people with eating disorders also have other related psychological difficulties, such as depression or anxiety, and may benefit from medications designed to help alleviate the symptoms of these problems. Your child may need to see a psychiatrist to obtain a prescription and to monitor the medication. Other specialists may also need to be involved, depending on the particular needs of your child and family.

A team approach to treatment means that each member of the team is focusing on the piece of the problem that is in his or her field of expertise. While this has its advantages, it can also make it difficult for you to keep track of various appointments and agendas. It is important to pick a therapist who can help you find the services your child needs and who is comfortable working with a team approach. Remember, two heads are better than one. In some cases, there may be many heads working together to figure out the best treatment strategies for your child. Keep in mind that although it can feel confusing to get one message from one doctor and a different message from another, each person on the treatment team has the same goal, to help you and your family with recovery. Take advantage of all the assistance they can provide!

How Much Will Therapy Cost?

As much as you are concerned about your child and want to do whatever you can to help him or her recover, you are probably also feeling a little nervous about the costs of therapy. This is a natural concern and need not be a cause for guilt. There are a number of factors that can affect the cost of therapy, including the type and training background of the therapist, the place where treatment occurs (such as private practice or a clinic), and the nature of the treatment (such as weekly outpatient visits or inpatient hospitalization). Factors specific to your family will also play a role in determining the costs of treatment, such as where you live, your income, and your insurance coverage. Because there are so many variables affecting how much therapy will cost, we encourage you to ask professionals and organizations in your area about their fees.

What Are the Treatment Options?

In addition to worrying about the costs of treatment, families often feel very confused about the vast array of psychotherapy services available. Psychotherapy is just a fancy word to refer to a session where you talk face-to-face with a therapist. This can happen in an individual (one-on-one) format or in a group format. Either method can be effective, and the choice of format depends in part on the services available to you and on your child's comfort level with talking to others about his or her problems. Although it may seem that your child will benefit less from group treatment because group therapy offers less individual attention, the research shows specialized group treatment for bulimia nervosa can be just as effective as individual treatment (Chen, in press). Group members provide motivation, suggestions, and support to one another.

Psychotherapy can be comprised of many different types of interventions and it is worthwhile to ask potential therapists what their theoretical orientation is and what research support exists to suggest that their approach is successful for treating eating disorders. There is no one right way to do therapy; different approaches work for different people and for different problems.

- *Behavior therapy.* In behavior therapy, you can expect the clinician to focus on altering patterns of behavior as well as aspects of the person's life situation to change the way he or she interacts with the environment. Examples of behavioral techniques include having clients try a food they have been avoiding or change their eating style by stocking their refrigerator so that only nutritious meals and snacks are available. Stress management and relaxation training may also be used to help people cope with negative feelings and life events.

- *Cognitive therapy.* Cognitive therapy is a related method (in fact, a common approach to treating eating disorders is called *cognitive behavioral therapy* or CBT). This type of therapy involves raising a client's awareness of the maladaptive thoughts and assumptions that contribute to distressing or unhealthy feelings and behaviors. Clients learn how to challenge and modify these thoughts.

- *Family therapy.* Family therapy may incorporate some of the techniques of the cognitive and behavioral approaches but also focuses on discussion and problem solving with every member of the family to determine how they can interact with each other in more supportive ways.

- *Interpersonal therapy.* Interpersonal therapy focuses on understanding how relationships with others and responses to life transitions or personal loss influence current behaviors, emotional well-being, and health.

- *Other treatments.* In addition to these structured approaches to treatment that focus specifically on current problems, there are also a variety of other techniques with different objectives. For example, psychoanalysis is usually a long-term therapy that tries to bring to light the role of past experiences and unconscious motivations on present difficulties.

- *Expressive therapy.* These therapies are often available in inpatient hospitals, day treatment programs, and residential treatment centers. The goal is to use movement, art, or music to help express emotions that are difficult to convey verbally.

While this is not an exhaustive list of all the different forms of therapy available, we hope that it gives you a sense of the vast array of interventions from which you can choose. Remember, there is more than one thing you can try. Keep in mind that it is important to ask if there is good research evidence to indicate that the approach you choose is successful for your child's particular set of problems.

Now that you have a sense of the types of therapy available and some of the issues involved in seeking treatment, we will turn to the more practical concern of how to find a therapist in your area to start the evaluation and treatment process.

Finding Treatment Referrals

Although it may feel like your family is very alone in facing this problem, there are a remarkable number of people in North America using mental health services, and you have many options available for a treatment referral:

- Your child's pediatrician or your own physician.

- Your local mental health association, which will be listed in the Yellow Pages, is another possibility. It is true that these state-funded services sometimes have a waiting list for services or particular eligibility criteria, but even if they cannot help you directly, they can serve as a good referral source.

- Another approach is to contact a national organization that services mental health in general, such as the National Mental Health Association or the American Psychological Association. Ask for eating disorder-specific referrals in your area.

- Don't forget the value of speaking to people whom you already know and trust to learn if they have a particular recommendation. If someone you know has a therapist they are happy with, this can be a great referral source.

- If you want to access an eating disorder specialist directly, we have included a list of Web sites and phone numbers that you can use to obtain more information (see Resources section). Keep in mind, however, that simply having a service provider listed on a Web site does not assure you of the therapist's effectiveness or the clinic's quality. You still want to use your own judgment.

- You may also consider speaking with your family physician, clergy person, or a school, family, or child guidance counselor. There are also local chapters of national agencies that provide services to anyone in need, such as Catholic Charities and Jewish Family and Children's Services.

Initially, these organizations may feel more familiar and comfortable for you, and they can serve as a good place to get you started. However, keep in mind the importance of ultimately finding a therapist who can treat the eating disorder. To learn about the training and background of different types of therapists (psychologists, psychiatrists, social workers, etc.), you can log on to the National Mental Health Association's Web site, which summarizes the main types of mental health professionals and their qualifications.

Depending on the size of the place where you live, there may be few or an astonishing number of referrals in your area. Although you may end up making a lot of phone calls before hitting on the right match for your family, try not to be discouraged. Once you have found a good resource, you can step back and share your fears and concerns about the illness with a professional who can help.

Questions to Ask a Provider

Once you have contacted a service provider and set up a time to meet for an initial evaluation, you may feel nervous: "Is this person going to blame me for my child's problem? Can this person actually help my child? Are they going to ask embarrassing questions or make me feel uncomfortable?" These concerns are common when people seek assistance with mental health for the first time. Thinking through the issues that are important to you will increase your comfort about going to the first session (or sending your child if he or she is going to be seen alone).

We have compiled a list of questions, modified from many different eating disorder and mental health resources, for you to consider. You do not need to find out the answers to all of these questions. Instead, think about which issues matter to you most and make those questions your priority. Feel free to address these questions to an individual therapist, a treatment facility or hospital, or other eating disorder support services that you contact. Also, after you get answers to these questions, if you feel uncomfortable, it is okay to let the therapist know that you want to think about it for a bit or talk with other potential therapists before making a decision. We recommend that you take notes on your conversations with providers.

Questions to Ask a Therapist

- "How long have you been treating eating disorders?"_____

_____

- "Do you have special training for working with these problems?" _____

_____

- "What are your training credentials?"_____

_____

Plan for the Evaluation

- "What kind of evaluation process will be used to formulate the treatment plan?" _____

_____

- "How long will it take?" _____

- "Will we have to wait before we can make the second appointment?" _____

- "Will my child be put on a wait list, following the evaluation, in order to be seen for treatment?"_____

- "What is the process for receiving feedback after the evaluation (for providing a diagnosis and recommending a treatment plan)?" _____

_____

- "Following the evaluation, will you or someone else conduct the treatment?" _____

- "If someone else, how will the referral work and will you still be involved with my child's care?" _____

Treatment Approach

- "What is your treatment style?" _____

- "Why do you think this approach will be helpful for my child?"

_____

- "What evidence is there that this approach is effective for treating eating disorders?" _____

_____

- "What are the typical recovery rates with this approach?" _____

_____

- "Are you used to working with other specialists, such as psychiatrists and dieticians, in treating eating disorders?" _____

_____

- "How does that work at this facility? For example, will my child need a medical evaluation before entering the program?" _____

_____

- "What do you suggest if my child doesn't want to participate in therapy, even though you and I both think he or she needs help?" _____

_____

- "Do you offer both individual and group therapy? Do you do family or couples therapy if necessary?" _____

_____

- "What is your policy about crises that occur in between sessions? For example, are you available for emergency sessions, or can I contact you between sessions if necessary, and is there an after-hours' number that I can use?" _____

_____

Expectations for Treatment

- "How long does treatment normally last and how do you know when it is time to stop treatment?" _____

_____

- "What are the benefits and the risks associated with the treatment plan you have recommended, and how does this compare with other treatment options?" _____

_____

_____

- "What role do family or friends play in the treatment?" _____

_____

- "What are the limits of confidentiality, both in general and regarding what you'll tell me about my child's treatment and progress?" _____

_____

- "How often do you usually talk to parents?" _____

_____

- "How frequently do you review progress, and how do you measure progress?" _____

_____

- "How can I best support my child during treatment, and what do you recommend I tell the rest of my family?" _____

_____

- "At what point do you recommend that a child be hospitalized? Is this based on weight or other factors, and how much of a role will I have in this decision?" _____

Business Issues

- "What is your appointment availability? Do you offer after-work or early morning appointments? How long do the appointments last? How often will you schedule sessions (with my child, with the rest of the family)?" _____

_____

_____

- "What are your fees, both for the evaluation and for individual or group therapy sessions?" _____

_____

- "How do I find out if you are reimbursable by my insurance, and what options do I have if I don't have mental health benefits under my health care plan?" (It is usually up to you to find out about your insurance coverage policy and the treatment alternatives that are available, but the provider can often help guide you regarding what you need to do.) _____

_____

- "Do you offer a sliding fee scale?" _____

- "Can the facility provide any written materials, such as information brochures, treatment plans, or a list of fees, so that I can have them for my own benefit and use them to explain the service to the insurance company?" _____

_____

You can also talk to the therapist about what he or she will expect of you and of your child, though this will usually be covered in the first couple of sessions. These expectations usually include guidelines about arriving on time for sessions and the cancellation policy. In addition, there are often assignments, like homework, that your child and the rest of the family may be asked to complete in between sessions to practice new skills. Your therapist will not expect these assignments to be completed perfectly, but therapy definitely requires a commitment and a fair degree of motivation to work through the hard times. The therapist may also ask that you or your child make a deal that you will talk to the therapist before you suddenly decide to drop out of treatment. While all therapists have their own style and guidelines, it is helpful to know in advance what everyone involved in the treatment should expect from each other. This can help you avoid misunderstandings and hurt feelings down the road.

Once your child has finished the first session, find out how comfortable she or he felt with the therapist, and also consider your own reaction. Do not expect to feel perfectly at ease the first time you meet someone, especially when you are being asked a lot of very personal questions! However, it is important that you feel that you were listened to and that the therapist behaved in a professional, trustworthy manner.

Also consider to what extent you, your child, and the therapist had similar goals for treatment.

Is the Internet a Valuable Resource?

The value of the Internet in accessing resources and information is tremendous. If you do not have access to the Internet at home or work, you can go to your local library. It allows you to find a wealth of information on eating and related disorders and provides tips on accessing treatment, support groups, and essentially every related topic. We recommend that you take advantage of this resource but with a cautious eye. The information on the Internet is not regulated or screened, so while there is an abundance of useful information available, there is also an excess of inaccurate, misleading, and even damaging material. Try to make the most of the resources at your fingertips, but also be aware of the range of accuracy of the material you come across. Here are some things you may want to think about as you surf the Internet for information about eating disorders and treatment:

- Consider the source of the posting. In most cases you can feel confident in the information posted at a government-run agency such as the National Institute of Mental Health or an organization that is led by professionals, such as the National Eating Disorders Association. While information posted on an individual's personal Web site may be useful, consider it no more valid than knowledge you have gained from talking to a stranger on a bus.

- Look to see whether the information presented and advice offered is supported by research or just by supposition. Caution: There are also individuals who post "pro-anorexia" sites on the Internet, and these are not only misleading but potentially harmful.

- If you see the same treatment strategy listed at four different eating disorder sites, you can have more confidence in its merit than if it is listed in only one place and not documented.

Making Your Home Recovery-Friendly

So far we have been writing with the assumption that you and your child are both motivated to seek professional help. We strongly hope that this is the case, but we also recognize that it may not be.

Regardless of whether or not your child has agreed to seek treatment, you should not feel like you are helpless to assist in your child's recovery. The research on how to prevent eating disorders from developing or worsening is still fairly new so there are many open questions. But there are also many ideas for you to try. There is no one right answer. We are going to provide you with a number of strategies that you can attempt to use with your child, and you can then monitor how effective each one is for your particular family situation. Not every strategy will work for every family. The important thing is to keep trying and to let your child know that you love and support him or her and have hope for recovery.

This chapter should reassure you that you can play an incredibly valuable role in your child's health and well-being, but this does not mean that you alone are expected to make your child better. Although it is natural for parents to believe it is up to them to control and fix their child's life, this is not a realistic belief when it comes to eating disorders. Ultimately, you cannot take full responsibility for either the problem or the solution of your child's illness. You cannot change your child's eating disorder behaviors—that is something your child has to do—but you can help to make things easier during this difficult time for your child, yourself, and other family members.

Strategies to Try

Given that there is not a lot of hard scientific evidence to guide recommendations for families, we have compiled a list of strategies from several sources. Some of these ideas come from our clinical experience as therapists working with young persons suffering with eating problems. Some of the suggestions are well-supported by research. And other recommendations have been compiled from a variety of books and Web sites that offer ideas about different approaches for family members.

This list is intended to provide you with lots of options to consider trying, but we do not expect every strategy to work for every family. Remember that the idea is not that you must follow each of these guidelines, but that you take a trial and error approach. For example, you may want to select three items from the list to try over the next two weeks. At the end of two weeks, check in to see how the change is affecting your child, yourself, and other family members. If you think the strategy is helpful, great; keep doing it. If not, decide whether you have given it a fair shot, or if you need to allow more time (for example, communication strategies, such as talking about emotions, can feel awkward at first and may require a longer trial period than is needed to change something like a daily meal schedule). If you feel you have made a reasonable effort to implement the strategy, but that it is not beneficial, then you should feel free to stop that tactic and select a new approach. The idea is that you continue to explore new ways of interacting as a family.

We have grouped the strategies into five categories for ease of reference: 1) responding to negative emotions, 2) managing food in the home, 3) setting a positive example, 4) having a life outside of the eating disorder, and 5) being open to treatment options. In reality, the ideas listed in one category will frequently draw upon skills from another category and will have diverse effects. So, you should not feel like you need to be limited to strategies from only one category, or that you have to pick ideas from every category. Start with the strategies that feel most approachable and the ones that you think could have the greatest impact on your child and family. You want to select an approach that feels as though it will be successful, especially at the beginning when you probably do not feel very confident. After that, you can try something a little harder. You can make some notes below on the relevance of different strategies for you, your child, and your family.

Responding to Negative Emotions

Although there are many ways to respond to a crisis, different approaches can be broadly categorized into two types of coping styles: those that are emotion focused and those that are problem focused. When you try to control the emotions surrounding a stressful situation, you are more emotion focused. You are more problem focused when you try to combat the problem (in this case, your child's illness) by attempting to address its underlying causes (Lazarus and Folkman 1984). People typically want to jump straight into the problem-focused style with the hopes that these efforts can make the problem go away, but managing negative emotions is also very helpful and needs to occur in tandem with the more practical strategies.

Try to not take your child's anger and behavior personally. It is not about you or even about your child's personality. These are symptoms of the eating disorder. They do not have to be tolerated and may need to have consequences, but understanding why they are happening can make a big difference. Always be clear that you are upset about a behavior. You can say that an action makes you angry, but do not communicate that your child is a bad person.

When your child is upset or engaging in unhealthy behaviors, take a moment to try to understand what he or she might be feeling, and write it down. What are some of the emotions he or she might be experiencing? Anger? Frustration? Sadness? Fear?

_____

_____

Try to avoid setting ultimatums. Declaring rules, such as "If I catch you bingeing one more time, no TV for a month," usually adds stress and guilt and does not alleviate the urges to binge or commit other harmful behaviors. It is likely that your child does not know how to inhibit his or her behavior at this point and will only feel worse if the pressure of an ultimatum is added to the already-present feelings of failure that are typical of eating disorders.

When you're feeling frustrated with your child and tempted to issue an ultimatum, try taking a short break from the stressful situation and check in with yourself about how you are feeling. What are your emotional reactions to your child's behavior? Write them down.

_____

_____

What are the possible consequences of giving an ultimatum? Write them down.

_____

_____

Don't pretend that the problem is not happening. Although your child may be reticent to discuss the eating disorder, you are not doing him or her any favors by denying its existence. Rather than ignoring the problem, encourage your child to have an evaluation and treatment if needed.

How can you express your concerns to let your child know that you care?

_____

_____

_____

Do not blame yourself. Eating disorders are caused by a multitude of factors, so feeling guilty and constantly criticizing yourself will only make you feel bad and will not help your child recover.

Managing Food in the Home

Inquiries about how to deal with food in the home and at mealtimes are some of the questions we are asked most frequently by our patients' families. Because of the importance of this topic, we go into more detail in chapter 5 about approaches you can try and nutritional guidelines for healthy eating. However, we have included some suggestions here so that you can start addressing these issues at home.

Try to avoid getting into power struggles over food. Attempting to force your child to eat or not to eat is likely to create enormous tension and bad feelings. It is also unlikely to be effective in the long run, because it encourages lying and more secretive behaviors. This does not imply that you do not set limits and offer no opinions. Rather, it means that you do not police the kitchen, yell at your child to finish her plate during dinner, or constantly ask your child what he or she has eaten that day.

Answer these questions in the space provided:

To what extent does my family already avoid power struggles over food?

_____

What are some examples of power struggles that have happened in my family?

_____

What are some ways to avoid these struggles?

_____

_____

What concrete changes can I make to reduce struggling with my child?

_____

_____

Ask your child for advice: Are there simple changes you can make in the family shopping (such as not buying a particularly tempting binge food) or in the preparation of meals (such as eating earlier so your child does not get too hungry) that would help him or her to manage the eating disorder more easily? Fill in the blanks:

Changes that can be made in shopping: _____

_____

Changes that can be made in the preparation of meals:_____

_____

Other changes that would help my child:_____

_____

_____

Make mealtimes pleasurable. Try to make sure you eat together as a family regularly (a few times a week if possible). By making dinner conversations sociable and enjoyable (do not use this time to talk about problems or discipline issues) and demonstrating that food can be enjoyed rather than feared, you can help to normalize your child's eating habits and beliefs. Encourage your child to join you at the table, even if she or he is not willing to eat the food you have prepared. You can come up with some good topics of conversation by thinking ahead. Fill in the blanks:

Fun topics of conversation:

_____

_____

Questions I have about my child's interests:

_____

_____

Things I'd like to know about my other children and/or spouse:

_____

_____

Stories I'd like to share with my family:

_____

_____

Other ways to make mealtimes more enjoyable:

_____

_____

Avoid linking food and eating with being a good or bad person. We tend to refer to certain foods as "bad" or "forbidden" (like chocolate and other "junk food"), turning food into a moral issue instead of a healthy, enjoyable part of each day. Along these lines, you should encourage healthy eating, rather than dieting. Promoting regular eating is very helpful. This means having three meals a day, a couple of snacks, and encouraging all members of your family to eat a variety of foods in moderation.

Ask yourself these questions:

"How has my own eating been lately? Have I had three meals a day and made healthy choices?"

_____

_____

"What changes can I make to promote healthy eating in my home?"

_____

_____

"What kinds of messages do I give about food and eating that I'd like to change?"

_____

_____

Setting a Positive Example

Parents often complain to us that their adolescent children only listen to their friends and do not pay any attention to what they say or do. While it is true that many young persons seem to work very hard to ignore their parents (and usually do exactly the opposite of what they recommend!), the research tells us that parents are actually extremely influential in modeling healthy food and exercise behaviors. Here are some things to do:

Demonstrate healthy ways to take care of yourself when you feel upset or stressed. For example, instead of turning to alcohol, drugs, or other destructive habits, try talking to family or friends about your feelings and problems, doing a fun and rewarding activity, or getting some relaxation or rest.

Write down some of the ways you can take care of yourself.

_____

_____

Instead of dieting, eat healthy balanced meals yourself. Show your child that food can be enjoyed and that our bodies regularly need food for fuel. Avoid referring to yourself as "bad" for eating a certain food. Become aware of whether you criticize your own body. Making self-critical remarks, like "Oh, I shouldn't have dessert" or "I feel so fat," sends your child a message that this is the way to think about food and weight. Talk to yourself about your body and your eating the way you hope your child will talk to him- or herself.

What are some positive comments you can make about eating:

_____

_____

What are some positive comments you can make about your body:

_____

_____

Be careful not to criticize your own or anyone else's body. Enjoy the fact that people come in all shapes and sizes. Instead of accepting the message from fashion magazines that only really thin people are beautiful, talk about the beauty of all different body types. Perhaps most importantly, talk about the qualities on the inside that really make a person beautiful, and make your child feel good about him- or herself as a person—not as a fashion model!

What are some positive comments you can make about your own personal attributes (that you are funny, hardworking, caring, etc.)?

_____

_____

Take care of your body by exercising regularly in moderation. This means promoting activity for the purposes of better health, not as a compulsive, driven competition to change your appearance. In fact, even overweight people who are physically active are healthier than thin people who are not fit. You can also tell your child that research indicates that being fit is more important for good health than being thin.

What are some exercises you enjoy?

_____

_____

Having a Life Outside of the Eating Disorder

A common but very unhealthy way that an eating disorder impacts a child's parents is by taking joy away from their lives. It is easy to have the eating disorder take over not only the child's life but the rest of your family's life as well. This leads to everyone becoming depressed and anxious and, as a consequence, less able to care for one another. One of the best things you can do for your child is take care of yourself! This means maintaining relationships and activities that are separate from the eating disorder and finding ways for you to relax and smile. Some parents feel guilty about enjoying themselves when their child is ill, thinking this means they are somehow uncaring. The truth is that maintaining your own physical and emotional health is an important factor in taking care of your child. Showing your child that life can be pleasurable can help motivate his or her recovery; it does not mean that you do not care about your child's suffering.

Maintain relationships with supportive friends and other family members. Avoid giving all of your attention to the child who is ill. While serious family illnesses can bring a family closer together, the stress and disruption can also push people apart. The advice and support of others can help put your child's illness into perspective and provide important distractions from the daily stresses of dealing with the disorder. This support for yourself will then enable you to provide more helpful care and support for your child because you will be better prepared to handle his or her sickness.

Make a list of family and friends who are supportive:

_____

_____

Find ways to alleviate the incredible stress you are under. This could mean participating in a relaxation program, like yoga, or doing some sort of regular activity with friends, like playing on a sports team or book club. You may also want to consider individual or couples counseling to help manage your pain; it is okay to acknowledge that the eating disorder is hurting you too, and not just your child.

Make a list of activities you enjoy:

_____ _____

_____ _____

_____ _____

_____ _____

Take breaks from dealing with the eating disorder. This means doing pleasurable activities with your child. You want to have as much of a normal life as possible; whenever you do spend fun time with your child (like going to a movie or for a walk), you are emphasizing the healthy parts of your relationship. This also reminds you both that there is a life outside the eating disorder. The entire day does not have to be consumed by sadness about your child's illness and trips to the doctor.

Make a list of fun family activities:

_____ _____

_____ _____

_____ _____

_____ _____

Being Open to Treatment Options

Seeking professional help for a mental health problem can be intimidating and feel uncomfortable. Many of us grew up with the belief that you do not "air your dirty laundry," or that a family member's problems should be kept private and not discussed outside of the family. Other people believe that if they or someone in their family has a problem, it is their responsibility to fix it and they should not accept help from an outsider. Still others feel ashamed because they imagine that seeing a therapist means they are crazy or that others will judge them negatively. Although these fears feel real, they are often inaccurate and can get in the way of recovery. We ask that you keep an open mind and remember that your child's eating disorder is a serious illness. It is not shameful, but does require specialized treatment.

Talk to your child about the value of treatment. Try to reduce your child's fears about the stigma of mental health care. At the Anorexia Nervosa and Related Eating Disorder Web site, they note that if a friend or family member had cancer, you would not hesitate to get the person the best professional care available. The same should be true in this case. In fact, eating disorders are sometimes called "soul cancer," and deserve to be treated with the same seriousness that you would treat physical cancer.

Help your child understand how the eating disorder is hurting him or her. It is common for people with eating problems to minimize the seriousness of the problem, and deny the need for treatment. One approach is to help your child with what psychologists call a "decisional balance," where you identify the pros and cons of the eating disorder so that the illness can be evaluated more objectively. For example, you can ask your child:

What are the advantages of eating the way you do? Make a list of the advantages.

_____

_____

_____

What are the disadvantages of eating the way you do? Make a list of the disadvantages.

_____

_____

_____

You can use this method to help your child learn to recognize the lack of energy, weakness, and difficulty concentrating that follows from restricting food intake.

You can also have discussions with your child about the ideas he or she has about the role that weight plays in life. Help your child to examine the thoughts he or she may have about the importance of weight and to understand that these ideas may not be realistic. For example, you may want to ponder the following questions with your child: What would life be like if you were the weight you want to be? Does being thin really make a person happy, successful, have good friends, do well in school, etc.?

The idea is to help your child see that the eating disorder is not getting your child the life that he or she wants, but instead is hurting his or her health, self-esteem, relationships, schoolwork, and happiness.

Listen to the advice from your child's caregivers. For example, if your child's doctor or therapist suggests hospitalization, consider this option very seriously; it may save your child's life. Also, be open to family or couples counseling if this is recommended. This does not mean that you will be blamed for the eating disorder. The purpose of this therapy is to help you interact more effectively as a family and handle the stress of the eating disorder in healthier ways.

Questions and Answers Now That You Know There's a Problem

Question: "Treatment sounds like a lot of stress and work. We haven't even begun this process and already we're stressed. I've heard that eating disorders sometimes just go away, so why don't we wait to see if the problem goes away before we get a therapist involved?"

Answer: The danger that the disorder will get worse if left untreated is far too great for you not to encourage treatment for your child at this time. For example, we know that treatment outcomes for eating disorders are most successful when the illness is treated early. In fact, treatment can often take longer if the person has had the disorder for a long time, and unfortunately, individuals who respond poorly to treatment are often those who have suffered with their illness for a longer period of time (Fahy and Russell 1993). Getting help early for young persons is especially important because this increases the chances that the child can avoid the often irreversible physical consequences of an eating disorder, such as stunted growth, delay of puberty, and increased risk for osteoporosis.

Although it is critical for your family to seek professional help as early as possible, we recognize that this is asking a lot. This is already a very stressful time for your family, and it can seem overwhelming to add a commitment that may be emotionally challenging, expensive, and time-consuming. What we ask is that you explore treatment options for your child. Ultimately, your level of involvement in the therapy will be up to you, your child, and the therapist that you select. Be up front about your concerns and the commitment you can make. There are no hard-and-fast rules about what parents need to do, but your child needs help as soon as is feasible.

Question: "I am so scared. I've heard that you can die from eating disorders. Maybe I should pull my daughter from school and her piano class because I don't want to add any stress to her life."

Answer: Different professionals have divergent perspectives on this issue because it seems that some people can recover while continuing their other activities while other young people need to make more drastic life changes to facilitate healing. Your daughter may be able to lead a relatively normal life while trying to recover. It might enable her to have areas of her life that she feels good about instead of feeling like the only thing present in her life is the eating disorder. However, for many people, high levels of stress increase the eating disorder symptoms. For this reason, we suggest that you monitor how outside activities, such as piano classes, impact the severity of the eating disorder. If you find that around the time of a recital your daughter becomes more ill, then this may be a sign that the piano classes are adding unhealthy stress to her life right now.

You can treat this as an experiment, perhaps suggesting to your daughter that if she wants to continue piano lessons, you will try this for six weeks, but then you will renegotiate to determine what role these extra activities are having on her health and recovery. Remind her that getting better is her most important job right now, and that once recovered, she can rejoin the piano class.

One important point to keep in mind is that piano lessons are very different from activities like ballet and gymnastics that emphasize body shape and weight. Research tells us that participation in these body-focused activities is a risk factor for the development of an eating disorder, so a break from these activities may be needed while your child is trying to recover (Byrne 2002). Strenuous athletic activities such as rowing or running may also pose a problem. We suggest that you ask your child's therapist whether stopping this activity (at least for a while) would be helpful. It can also be useful to ask your child how she feels about herself and her body when she is in ballet class to learn what effect the class has on her.

Question: "My daughter wants to keep this a secret, but I feel like that makes me a liar if I don't tell the rest of the family. What should I do?"

Answer: Given the secrecy associated with eating disorders, it is common for people to want no one to know about their illness. While we recommend that you respect your daughter's wishes and privacy in general, the effects of secrecy and shame can be damaging to the rest of the household and can lead to confusion, hurt feelings, and misunderstandings. For this reason, we generally find it important that if there are two parents in the household or in the child's life, both parents know about the eating disorder and have a shared plan about how they will respond to the symptoms. If not, the child will receive mixed messages, and the secrecy is bound to create tension in the parent relationship.

With respect to siblings or other members of the household, we encourage you to ask your child to agree to a family meeting where the others are told at least some information about her being sick and struggling with food. It is not necessary to go into great detail about the eating disorder, but all family members are being affected by the illness, so telling them how they can help is important. Otherwise, they may feel resentful of the special treatment the sick child is receiving or confused that certain foods (like junk food that your daughter may use for binges) are no longer available in the home. In this meeting, it will be important to emphasize to the other siblings your daughter's wish to not share information about her illness with other people. This is a challenging balance because you want to respect your daughter's right to some privacy, but you also do not want to encourage the idea that the eating disorder is shameful and should be kept a secret.

Question: "Our eight-year-old child wants to know why her sister is sick. What am I supposed to tell her? She's already talking about going on a diet so she can be just like her big sister!"

Answer: You can talk to your child in an age-appropriate way to answer her questions. For example, you can explain that the older daughter is sick because she is not eating well and that the best way the eight-year-old child can help is by eating healthy meals with the rest of the family. Explain that while you think it is wonderful that she admires her big sister, she should not try to copy all of her sister's behaviors, because dieting is dangerous and she needs to eat nutritious foods to grow.

Rebecca's Story

Rebecca, a seventeen-year-old student at a competitive private school, began restricting her food intake and exercising a lot in the spring of her senior year. Her parents noticed that she had lost some weight, but it didn't seem like her behaviors were too extreme, and she explained to them that she was just trying to get into shape in time for college. What her parents did not know was that Rebecca had begun vomiting. After a few months of this behavior, she confessed to one of her teachers that she was getting out of control and was scared. The teacher wanted to help Rebecca, but Rebecca begged her not to tell her parents, as she was sure they would not understand. Although Rebecca was convincing in her plea not to involve her parents, when the teacher and school principal discussed the situation, they agreed that because Rebecca was still a minor and living at home, they needed to let her parents know what was going on.

Rebecca and her parents sat down with the principal and the teacher and had a frank discussion about it. Although Rebecca was upset at the time, she did agree to try to see a therapist with her parents and get some help. The first couple of meetings with the therapist were difficult. Rebecca was angry that she was not able to "handle this on her own," and yet she found the therapist to be empathic and knowledgeable about eating disorders. The therapist worked at a specialized eating disorder clinic, and they decided that she would be Rebecca's therapist, while another psychologist on the staff would work with the family. This allowed Rebecca to have a private relationship with her therapist and also have the opportunity to have family sessions where they could discuss how the family environment could be changed to help her recovery.

Colleen's Story

Colleen's eating disorder started during her first year of high school. She would stay up late at night doing homework while her family was asleep, and her breaks from studying involved lots of snacking. Upset by her eating and worried about gaining weight, Colleen felt very guilty after bingeing and quickly learned to vomit, which she thought was an effective way to manage her weight. One year later, she was bingeing and purging three times a week and feeling increasingly out of control. She wanted help to stop this pattern.

Although both of her parents knew about her eating disorder by the time she started therapy, Colleen was reluctant to have them involved in treatment. She felt ashamed about her eating and wanted to take care of it herself. However, during the first weeks of sessions, Colleen and her therapist identified a number of problematic situations in the home that were contributing to her bingeing and purging. For example, Colleen's favorite binge foods included ice cream and cookies. Although she thought that she might have an easier time reducing her bingeing and purging if these foods were not in the house, she felt unable to make this request of her parents. Her father enjoyed having dessert in the evenings, and she believed that it would not be fair to deprive him of foods that he liked. After much discussion about the pros and cons of having a meeting with her parents and therapist to discuss this, Colleen agreed to include her parents in a session to talk about the family shopping list and types of foods available in the house.

Colleen was nervous and fidgety when she arrived for the family session with both of her parents. With encouragement, Colleen told her parents about the foods that were particularly risky for her and talked about feeling worried about asking that these foods be excluded from the family's grocery list. Her mother expressed concern about Colleen's level of worry and asked for more information about foods that were risky for her. And, much to Colleen's surprise, her father did not insist on keeping snack foods in the house or express disappointment about not having ice cream and other binge foods on the shopping list. Instead, he remarked that he had noticed how quickly ice cream was disappearing from the freezer but felt uncomfortable talking with her about this. He had been worried about Colleen's eating habits for some time and had been thinking about not having foods such as ice cream at home but was afraid that she would be opposed to this. After discussing this, the family agreed to keep certain high-risk snacks out of the house in order to reduce the availability of binge foods for Colleen.

With the assistance of the therapist, Colleen and her family were able to come to an agreement fairly easily. However, this session drew attention to their difficulties in communicating with one another at home. The therapist recommended that Colleen and her parents have discussions more frequently in addition to regularly reviewing their decision to keep binge foods out of the house. Throughout the course of the next two months, Colleen's parents eliminated binge foods from their shopping list, which helped decrease Colleen's bingeing and purging.

Creating Solutions

We know that finding a therapist and making changes in your home are both very difficult, especially when your family is under stress and used to handling problems in a certain way. To help you, we have put together two worksheets to get things started.

Finding the Right Therapist for Your Family

Have you spoken to your child about contacting a therapist?

_____

_____

What was the result of this conversation? _____

_____

_____

What type of therapist do you want to contact first? (psychologist, family therapist?) _____

Have you prioritized the questions you want to ask on the phone, and before and after the initial evaluation? _____

Using the resource list at the end of this book (or a referral from someone you know), who do you want to contact first? _____

_____

Outcome: Has an appointment been set? How comfortable do your child and you feel with this therapist? _____

_____

_____

If you are not happy with this first contact, who will you try next?

_____

Outcome: _____

_____

_____

Next step:_____

Congratulations on finding a therapist for your child!

Selecting Strategies to Make Changes at Home

What strategy feels like it would be feasible to implement in your household? How would you go about doing this?_____

_____

_____

What strategy feels like it would be helpful for you, your child, or the rest of the family? What changes do you expect to see if this strategy works? _____

_____

_____

What barriers or obstacles might you encounter in implementing this strategy? How can you plan ahead to try to prevent these problems?

_____

_____

How will you remind yourself to try this strategy? Should you schedule it for a certain time of day, write a note on the refrigerator, tell other people, or come up with another reminder?_____

_____

_____

When will you check in to see whether this strategy has been helpful? How will you decide whether to keep trying it or move on to try something new? _____

_____

_____

_____

Monitoring Your Progress

Selected Strategy	Outcome	Plan for Next Step
1. _____	_____	_____
_____	_____	_____
2. _____	_____	_____
_____	_____	_____
3. _____	_____	_____
_____	_____	_____
4. _____	_____	_____
_____	_____	_____
5. _____	_____	_____
_____	_____	_____

CHAPTER 3

How Did This Happen?
Understanding the Causes of Eating Disorders

When I think about my daughter's eating disorder, I just keep asking myself how did this happen to her? She's attractive, smart, and seems to succeed at everything she does. Has she been unhappy for years and we just didn't know it? I feel like I don't even know my own child anymore.

—Sheila, mother of a sixteen-year-old girl
with anorexia nervosa

Once the diagnosis has been made and you are certain that your child has an eating disorder, you may begin to struggle with the question of how this happened. Why *your* child? Why *your* family? It's normal to feel confused, angry, scared, embarrassed, and even guilty. Some parents worry about comments that they made to their children and question how food, eating, and body weight issues were handled in the family. We believe it is useful to think about the past, but that it is not helpful to become overwhelmed with guilt and remorse about previous events. Parents who have encouraged dieting may feel particularly remorseful. It is important to realize, however, that no single event or comment sets off an eating disorder.

There are multiple causes of eating disorders. For any given individual, a combination of personal, biological, and environmental factors, as well as life events, can contribute to the emergence of an eating problem. While it may be frustrating not to be able to point to one specific reason, this also means that no one person or event is to blame.

In this chapter, we address myths about the causes of eating disorders and provide information about the true contributing factors. We also outline professional theories on how eating disorders develop so that you can use these perspectives to generate ideas about your child's situation. We answer common questions families ask us about where eating disorders come from and provide case examples so you can see how other families handled difficult situations. Finally, we help you to identify the risk factors that may have contributed to your child's eating disorder.

Debunking Myths about the Causes of Eating Disorders

Myth: Parents are responsible for causing their child's eating disorder.

Research says: There is no one cause of an eating disorder and it is not helpful for parents to blame themselves. As we stated earlier, researchers have found that disordered eating is often the result of a number of biological, social, psychological, and environmental factors (Schmidt 2002). No one family type is responsible for the onset of an eating disorder (Rastam and Gillberg 1991), and in fact, families can help play an important role in helping their child to recover.

The research evidence is mixed about what characteristics typify families where a child develops an eating disorder. Some studies have found that families of children with eating disorders (compared to families of children without eating problems) are more likely to avoid conflict, have unrealistically high expectations for their children, and be overly dependent on one another (Eisler 1995). Other studies have found no support for the idea of a typical anorexia nervosa family (Rastam and Gillberg 1991). These conflicting findings suggest that blanket generalizations about families are not accurate or fair.

Parents and children influence one another in multiple ways over the years. It is not productive to blame either children or parents for the onset of an eating disorder. Instead, you should focus on how to address your child's eating disorder in a direct and honest way today.

Myth: Children with eating disorders were sexually abused.

Research says: Trauma and negative life events, in general, increase the risk of developing a variety of emotional and psychological difficulties. Research suggests that any form of abuse (physical, sexual, or psychological) increases the risk for developing a range of psychological problems, which include eating disorders (Pope and Hudson 1992). However, there is not a direct relationship between abuse and eating disorders: Not all people with eating disorders were abused, and not all people who were abused develop an eating disorder. Although sexual abuse may be a factor in the onset of eating problems, it is not a unique contributor to the development of eating disorders (Pope and Hudson 1992).

Eating disorders often serve as a way to cope with stress and negative feelings. For example, some people think that excessively restrictive dieting in anorexia gives children the false impression that they are exerting control over their life and their environment. Similarly, it is believed that the binge-purge cycle in bulimia nervosa may help young people temporarily escape from life's problems (Heatherton and Baumeister 1991). Stress associated with major life events, such as the death of a family member, parental divorce or unemployment, or moving to another city increases a young person's risk for developing an eating disorder. A similar increase in risk occurs during important life transitions, such as puberty, leaving home, or starting college.

Myth: My son has an eating disorder, so he must be gay.

Research says: It is only partially true that homosexuality is a risk factor for eating disorders among males. It is estimated that approximately 20 percent of males suffering from an eating disorder are homosexual, which is higher than the rates of homosexuality among males in the general population (Andersen 2002). Still, the majority of men with eating disorders are heterosexual.

Some research indicates that homosexual males place a greater emphasis on physical appearance and report higher levels of body dissatisfaction than heterosexual males do (Siever 1994). This suggests that sexual orientation is not the key factor putting a person at risk for developing an eating disorder. Instead, the key factor here is the unhealthy preoccupation with shape and weight, and this preoccupation can occur for anyone, regardless of gender or sexuality.

What Are the Common Causes of Eating Disorders?

It is natural to wonder why your child developed an eating disorder, but there is probably no simple answer because a number of diverse factors can lead to the onset of disordered eating. The goal is to understand these factors and consider how to respond to them, rather than cast blame. These factors fall into seven broad categories:

Society

Societal factors seem to play a large role in the development of eating disorders, as there are higher rates of eating disorders in Western societies than in other cultures. During the latter half of the twentieth century, thinness was equated increasingly with beauty, as well as wealth and competence (Hsu 1989). At the same time, there has been a growing discrepancy between society's ideals of beauty and weight norms, as people's average weight has stayed the same or increased. This ideal of thinness can cause people of normal weight to feel unhappy and dissatisfied with their bodies.

Our society has come to value thinness and to believe that thin is better. We hold irrational beliefs that being thin is symbolic of being capable and in control, while being overweight is linked to being out of control and indulgent. Much of this irrational and unfair thinking stems from messages expressed through the media. Movies, television, and magazine ads all bombard us with images of thin, successful people and suggest that all it takes is willpower to look like a super model! As a result, adolescents, in particular, are often willing to go to extreme lengths to achieve the "ideal" thin body, even though in most cases it is physically impossible to attain this image and remain healthy (Brownell 1991). This problem is worsened by the fact that for many adolescents, body image and self-esteem are closely linked. So, the discrepancy between the ideal body and their actual body makes young people feel terrible about themselves. This can prompt extreme dieting, which can lead to the onset of an eating disorder.

Life Events

Research suggests that a buildup of life stressors can predispose a person to eating problems. Though no one single experience can cause an eating disorder, the following events have often been cited as precursors to unhealthy eating:

- major life transitions, such as puberty, starting a new school, or entering adulthood

- problems with communicating in the family

- changing roles or difficulty adjusting to increased responsibility

- problems in social or romantic relationships

- traumatic life events

- the presence of other psychological illnesses (such as depression, substance abuse, anxiety and personality disorders)

These factors don't cause eating disorders by themselves, but they can increase the likelihood that a vulnerable person will develop an eating problem. Consider which of these risk factors may be relevant for your child, as it may help you address problems due to life events in the process of recovery.

Individual Factors

Similar to life events, there is no one characteristic about an individual that will determine whether or not he or she will develop an eating disorder, but the following factors are frequently seen among children and adolescents with eating problems:

- high self-expectations/perfectionism

- poor body image

- extreme need for approval

- tendency to think in black-and-white terms

- low self-esteem

- feelings of anxiety and sadness

Research suggests that certain personality characteristics are common among people with eating disorders. In anorexia nervosa, these characteristics include high levels of restraint and inhibition, a desire to conform, perfectionism, avoidance of risk-taking, and a dependence on outside rewards and compliments as sources of self-worth. In bulimia nervosa, these traits include interpersonal sensitivity and an outgoing personality, as well as impulsivity, low emotional stability, and low self-esteem. Other research suggests that individuals with eating disorders have difficulty communicating their feelings, referred to as *alexithymia*. As a result, they engage in unhealthy eating behaviors as a way of coping with negative emotions (Schmidt, Jiwany, and Treasure 1993).

You may have heard that eating disorders are more common among gay males and less common among lesbian women. These statements are only partially true. As stated above, there are more homosexual males in groups of males with eating disorders (compared to males without eating disorders), but most males with eating disorders are not gay. Among lesbian women, the incidence of eating disorders is believed to be lower than among straight women, but recent research indicates that lesbian women are not immune to eating disorders. Many lesbian females struggle with unhealthy attitudes about their bodies and a preoccupation with shape and weight (Beren, et al. 1996), putting them at risk for developing an eating disorder just like the rest of the female population.

Negative Influences from Family and Friends

Due to cultural pressures to be thin, an unfortunate norm exists where the vast majority of people do not feel satisfied with their bodies. Without even realizing it, friends and family may make negative comments about eating, shape, and weight that can be very painful for individuals who are vulnerable to developing eating problems. These negative influences from friends and family can come in a number of different forms.

When parents complain about their own bodies or about another family member's body, children learn that they will be evaluated based on their appearance, instead of on more important characteristics, such as who they are as a person. Making comments such as "I look fat in this dress" can make a child who already has eating concerns worry that she also looks fat or worry that you will think poorly of her if she gains weight. Think about what your casual comments imply about what traits you value in yourself and other people.

Children learn about healthy eating in part based on family behavior at the dinner table. Be wary of making comments about foods being "good" or "bad" or people being good or bad, based on what they eat. Food should not be treated as a moral issue. Instead, the goal should be to make healthy eating a priority. This means showing your children how to eat a balanced diet (see chapter 5) and teaching them that eating three meals a day plus snacks is important. We also suggest that you be careful not to criticize family members about what they are eating and how much—you do not want to make food a control issue and turn meal times into a battleground. Instead, we recommend that you provide lots of healthy eating options and fewer unhealthy ones, so that your children can learn from you how to enjoy healthy food choices and take care of their bodies.

Avoiding negative comments about shape, weight, and eating is especially important in families where some members are obese, because this can make an individual more vulnerable to unhealthy eating patterns. Remember to focus on nutritious eating and, if your family is going to comment on appearance, try to make positive comments about one another and yourself. No one should be made to feel bad about their body—it is up to us to teach children that people can be beautiful in all different shapes and sizes.

Peer pressure can also negatively influence a child's eating patterns. For example, friends who make hurtful comments about their own bodies or your child's body, as well as friends who evaluate others based upon appearance only (rather than more meaningful characteristics), can make a child feel that he or she has to be thin to be accepted. In this way, school cafeterias can often be very difficult places for an individual with eating concerns, since other kids who do not eat in healthy ways and who focus on dieting may place pressure on vulnerable adolescents to copy these unhealthy behaviors. Again, you can help by encouraging your children to spend time with friends who make them feel good about themselves and teaching them strategies to resist negative peer pressure.

It is also important to check in with your children about their perceptions of your behavior and comments. Unfortunately, adolescents are especially prone to misunderstandings and often interpret comments in negative ways. So, even if you think that a remark you made was positive, it is worth checking to make sure that you and your child understood one another.

If you have not been talking with your child in these ways, try to be patient with yourself as you learn new ways of communicating. Also, keep in mind that there is no one right way for families to interact. But you can always try something new.

Unhealthy Eating Patterns

It is common to see patterns of unhealthy eating before the onset of a full eating disorder. It seems that weight gain coupled with social reinforcement of the thinness ideal may cause a child to begin dieting or to intensify dieting attempts. Dieting can also be triggered by stressful life events, such as family problems and school worries. Unfortunately, such dieting puts an individual at a greater risk for developing an eating disorder. For example, the restraint of food intake that accompanies dieting often leads to bingeing, which can in turn contribute to the onset of an eating disorder, such as bulimia or binge eating disorder. Beyond its effects on our behavior, food deprivation can have profound psychological effects, such as depression, anxiety, rigid obsessive thinking, and social withdrawal (Keys, et al. 1950).

Self-Defeating Thoughts

People who suffer from eating disorders sometimes engage in certain patterns of distorted (and often self-critical) thinking that may contribute to their illness. These are known as cognitive distortions. In trying to understand your child's behavior, it may be helpful for you to consider some examples of these thoughts. Behaviors that initially seem irrational make more sense when you consider the self-defeating thoughts that drive them. The categories listed below, adapted from the *Handbook of Treatment for Eating Disorders*, demonstrate some of the common reasoning errors among people with eating disorders (Garner, Vitousek, and Pike 1997):

All-or-nothing thinking (thinking in black-and-white terms)

- "If I eat one potato chip, I may as well eat the whole bag."

- "If my waist gets one inch bigger, I'll keep eating until it's gigantic."

Overgeneralizations (making sweeping negative conclusions)

- "I used to be ten pounds heavier than I am now and I was miserable, so I know that gaining weight will make me depressed."

- "If I make one mistake, it means I am a total failure."

Magnification (magnifying the negative aspects of a situation)

- "I've gained three pounds, so I can't possibly show myself at the beach."

- "If someone thought I was fat, I would just die."

Superstitious Thinking (imagining negative consequences)

- "If I can just stay thin, my problems at school will go away."

- "If I eat at night, it will be instantly converted into fat on my thighs."

Personalization (assuming other people's behavior is about you)

- "When I see someone refuse dessert at a restaurant, I know they think I shouldn't have dessert either."

- "My friend didn't want to go out with me this weekend—I bet it's because I gained five pounds."

Selective Abstraction (focusing on a negative detail, instead of the whole picture)

- "I can only be a self-sacrificing person if I give up junk food."

- "Three guys asked me to dance tonight, but the guy I really liked didn't even look at me. I know it is because I am so fat."

It may be difficult to accept that your child actually has these thoughts. We included this list so that you can begin to understand why seemingly self-defeating behaviors, such as bingeing and vomiting, may occur.

When your child expresses these distorted beliefs, we encourage you to try to be supportive and understanding. It is usually not very effective to argue with someone in an effort to change his or her ideas, and it can make your child feel even worse about him- or herself. Instead, you can respond by reinforcing the idea that you value your child as a person and avoid engaging in a debate about his or her negative thoughts about shape and weight. You can clarify, however, that you do not share his or her negative beliefs.

In reading this list, you may also find that you have had some of these thoughts yourself. If that is the case, take some time to question your own beliefs. You may want to consider talking with a trusted friend or therapist to see if you are falling into the trap of distorting reality and making yourself feel bad.

Biological Factors

Eating disorders tend to run in families. Researchers have found that anorexia nervosa and bulimia nervosa appear to be several times more common among relatives with these disorders than in the general population. We still do not know how people inherit this vulnerability. If your family has an increased biological risk, this does not mean that there is nothing you can do to help your child (Strober and Bulik 2002). Instead, it should make you more watchful for warning signs of eating problems (discussed in chapter 1) and extra careful to promote healthy eating in your family.

There is no one single cause for an eating disorder. Just as the family is not to blame, you should also keep in mind that your child is not doing these self-injurious behaviors on purpose. The focus should be on how you can help to reduce the impact of those relevant risk factors to promote health and recovery for your child.

Professional Views: Theories on How Eating Disorders Develop

There are a few major psychological theories that have informed the treatment of eating disorders and are important to mention. As you read through each theory, think about which points feel most consistent with your perceptions of your child and your family.

We will review four theoretical perspectives: the cognitive behavioral view, the feminist view, the interpersonal view, and the psychodynamic view. Each of these perspectives comes out of a well-developed school of thought that informs the treatment of many different types of problems, but we will focus only on the application of these theoretical perspectives to eating disorders. In seeking out a therapist, it is a good idea to ask about his or her training and theoretical orientation so that you can understand how the therapist might approach your child's treatment. Some therapists integrate more than one of these perspectives into their treatment plan.

The Cognitive Behavioral View

The cognitive behavioral perspective takes the view that most people who develop eating disorders started off by going on an extreme diet. The theory is that the behavior and thoughts associated with trying to drastically restrict your food intake can eventually lead to binge eating. People who might be at particularly high risk for extreme dieting include those who have a career or hobby that demands a specific body type (like ballet, gymnastics, wrestling, equestrian, modeling, or acting) and those who also have some of the other personality and life factors discussed earlier in this chapter. Overrestrictive dieting includes behaviors such as skipping meals, completely avoiding certain foods, and the belief that certain foods are "bad."

Diets that involve total avoidance of certain foods contribute to the likelihood of binge eating through a phenomenon psychologists call "the abstinence violation effect" (Brownell, et al. 1986). The abstinence violation effect occurs when people decide to avoid a particular type of food (such as cake) and then find themselves in a situation where eating that food feels unavoidable (like at a birthday party). After eating a normal portion of the food, they feel that they have blown it and may as well eat a lot of it. This binge eating behavior can be attributed to "all-or-nothing" thinking, such as "If I can't be perfect, I may as well not try to restrain at all." Another common response in this situation is to plan to resume the diet tomorrow, so it makes sense to enjoy the forbidden foods today. After a binge episode, the person feels guilty and remorseful. Their dieting typically becomes even more rigid, which perpetuates the diet-binge cycle.

Here are some questions for you and your family to consider, as you think about the role that extreme dieting plays in your life:

Is eating a stressful or enjoyable time in your family?

_____

_____

How often do you skip meals?

_____

Do you try to make sure that meals include a variety of foods from the different food groups (e.g., meat, dairy, fruits and vegetables, grains, fats and oils, etc.)?

_____

_____

Does your family think of some foods as '"bad" or "forbidden"? Are there foods that you absolutely never have because you think they would cause you to gain weight? Do you believe that all foods are okay in moderation?

_____

_____

How often does your family encourage one another to diet or follow rigid rules about what or when to eat? To what extent do you monitor the size of each other's portions at the dinner table?

_____

_____

The Feminist View

The feminist view focuses on the ways in which our society creates unequal expectations and opportunities for the two genders and looks at how these different expectations and opportunities play a role in the development of eating disorders, especially among young girls. To explain the current rise in eating disorders, the feminist theorists consider the impact of the messages of our culture, both in the past and in the present. Societies have historically told women (particularly of the upper classes) that they need to go to painful extremes to be attractive. For example, beginning in the tenth century, Chinese women bound their feet tightly to keep them small, and as a result were crippled and unable to work or walk. In the nineteenth century, women wore corsets to create an unnaturally small waist, and this led to digestive problems and weakness. In our culture today, women are encouraged to diet, exercise, wear makeup, do their hair, wear fashionable clothes, and even get plastic surgery in order to appear young, thin, and attractive.

Even in the last fifty years, there has been a significant shift in the "ideal" body shape and size for women. For example, Marilyn Monroe was considered to be the beauty ideal of her time, yet she was much larger and more voluptuous than the typical actresses and models you see today. Research studies have examined the weights of Miss America contestants and *Playboy* centerfolds over the last several decades and have documented a substantial decrease in their typical weight (Wiseman, et al. 1992).

Feminist theory tries to explain why eating disorders occur more often in girls than boys and why these problems often emerge during adolescence. According to this approach, when adolescent girls begin to mature physically, they are actually moving away from the current ideal, which is very childlike, thin, and androgynous (neither very masculine nor feminine). This causes distress for the adolescent girl because she does not want to lose the body that looks more like the models she sees in magazines and on TV, and she desperately tries to retain her thin, childlike shape. In contrast, when boys mature, they become bigger and more like the ideal male body type (which in our society is very large and muscular).

Cultural messages have an impact on all of us. Here are some questions for you and your family to consider, as you think about the role cultural messages play in your lives.

How do you feel when you see very thin or very muscular models in magazines? Does it make you feel better or worse about yourself?

_____

_____

What different responsibilities do the males and females in your household carry? Do you think this affects your male and female children's view of themselves?

_____

_____

What measures have you (or family members) tried to make changes in your appearance? What impact has this had?

_____

_____

What kinds of things have you wanted to do, but thought you could or should not do because of your gender? Now, think about someone of the opposite gender—what things might they have been inhibited to do because of their gender? What do you think about that?

_____

_____

The feminist view would encourage you to take action and not just accept the negative messages from the media that tell us how we have to look and behave because of our gender. Here are some suggestions:

Know the facts and discuss them with your family. Women's magazines have over ten times more articles and advertisements promoting weight loss compared to magazines geared toward men (Andersen 2002). Media images can influence the way you see yourself. Research has found that the amount of time we spend watching soap operas, movies, and music videos is linked to negative feelings about our bodies (Tiggeman and Pickering 1996).

Encourage your child to be a critical viewer of the media (adapted from the National Eating Disorders Association Web site, NEDA 2001). Remember that media images and messages are creations designed to sell us specific ideas or products. They do not reflect reality. Most women and men do not look like the people we see on TV. Particularly for women, no matter how much dieting or plastic surgery we have, our bodies are not meant to look like those models. In fact, most models have their pictures electronically altered, so even they do not look like that in real life! Here are some tips on how you can deal with unrealistic images of thinness and beauty in the media. These strategies are helpful for all members of your family (including you!), and it will be especially valuable to talk with your child about these ideas:

- Decide how you want to value yourself or others–choose to value the inside of a person, not the outside. Now apply that same rule to yourself, and challenge your children to do the same.

- When you hear or read something on television or in a magazine that makes you feel bad about yourself, *talk back*. Encourage your child to talk back to the television, or write a letter to the editor and producer letting them know the things that upset you. For example, you and your child can ask to see a greater range of body shapes represented in the media.

- When you see a program or advertisement that does make your family feel good, also let the editor or producer know. Your voices matter, so tell media representatives when you like things and when you do not.

- If a magazine ad is making you or your child feel miserable, just tear it out. You are not obligated when you read magazines for pleasure to look at things that make you feel less valuable as a person. Encourage your child to do the same.

- Talk to others about the effects of the media messages (especially your children); ask how they feel and suggest you take action together. This can include writing letters and watching television shows together so that you can talk about the unrealistic images that the media promote. Or, you can make a list of companies who consistently send belittling or negative messages about body shape and size, and then try to avoid buying their products (Maine 2001).

The Interpersonal View

The interpersonal view considers eating disorders in terms of how the child's past experiences influence present relationships and feelings of connection with others. According to this theory, if people have experiences where they do not feel adequately understood or cared for, they may develop the belief that others cannot be trusted or counted on for help.

Children who have these negative experiences may develop low self-esteem and worry a lot about how others view them. They may want very much for others to approve of them and try very hard to present themselves in a positive light. Because they feel like they are presenting a fake image to the outside world, they may end up feeling depressed, sad, angry, and lonely. They may then attempt to cope with these difficult feelings by binge eating, which helps them "numb out," or not feel these negative emotions even if only for a brief period of time.

The interpersonal view is similar to the *psychodynamic perspective* (discussed next), but it focuses more on current relationships and changes that can be made now.

Here are some questions to consider in terms of how food fits in with your family's personal relationships and emotional responses. Consider how both you and your child might respond to these issues. This is a good opportunity for each family member to think about which aspects of their relationships with food they like and which they would like to change:

When you feel sad or depressed about a loss, are you likely to eat more or less? What about your children?

Do you or your children have particular foods that you use for comfort or as a reward following a hard day?

Alternatively, have you ever felt you were punishing yourself by eating foods that are not healthy for you? How do your children think about food as a reward or punishment?

How often do you or other family members eat when lonely, angry, frustrated, nervous, upset, or worried?

How often does your eating feel out of control following an argument or other emotional event? What might your children say?

Does eating ever feel like an escape from your worries, a chance for you to "numb out" and not feel anything at all? Does eating make you feel better right away? Does the good feeling last? For an hour, three hours, a day? Does the eating ever make you feel worse about yourself? How about other family members?

The Psychodynamic View

Psychodynamic theories usually focus on how early life experiences influence a person's sense of self and his or her approach to the world. This view has a rich history, as it emerged from the work of Sigmund Freud and his recognition that experiences both within and outside of awareness can influence behavior. One of the objectives of psychodynamic therapy is to examine the past in order to illuminate the problems of the present.

Like the interpersonal view, the psychodynamic perspective includes the idea that a negative self-image, or low self-esteem, can contribute to eating disorders. For example, a young woman who does not feel good about herself may rely on weight loss to feel a sense of uniqueness or accomplishment. A popular and well-researched way to evaluate self-esteem is to use the Rosenberg Self-Esteem Scale (Rosenberg 1965). This test consists of a series of statements to which you are asked to respond, indicating the degree to which you agree or disagree. The statements, such as "I wish that I could have more respect for myself," "I feel that I am a person of worth, at least on an equal basis with others," and "I feel I do not have much to be proud of," each express high or low self-esteem. The scale evaluates your self-esteem, based on how you respond.

Do you think low self-esteem may be contributing to your child's difficulties? Keep in mind that having low self-esteem may be both a consequence of having an eating disorder as well as a potential contributing cause. Use this opportunity to talk with your child and brainstorm activities that your child might do to feel better about him- or herself. What does your child feel he or she is good at? What does she or he enjoy? Are there activities you can do together?

Questions and Answers about Causes of Eating Disorders

Question: "I read in a book that it's usually an overprotective mother and distant father that causes their child to get sick, but we raised both our girls the same way, and one has anorexia and the other one is fine."

Answer: It is common for children raised in the same family to have different responses to their environment. After all, the family style interacts with each child's unique personality, so kids and parents affect each other. In fact, the idea that there is a certain "type" of family that causes disordered eating in children is largely unsupported. The important thing to keep in mind is that you can be a valuable part of your daughter's recovery, and that it is not helpful for you to blame yourself for her becoming sick.

In addition, most of the research studies investigating family factors that contribute to eating disorders are conducted after the onset of the illness, so it is not clear whether these family patterns contributed to the development of an eating disorder or whether they occurred in response to the stress from a family member having an eating problem. In either case, the purpose of recognizing these difficult family interaction patterns is not to cast blame, but to think about how your family wants to interact in the future to help your child recover.

Question: "Do you think I should take away all fashion magazines from my children while my older daughter is in recovery? If they're a bad influence, maybe I should hide them."

Answer: There is no definite right or wrong answer here, but there is now evidence indicating that fashion magazines that are overloaded with slick images of very thin women can make young women feel insecure about themselves. One strategy is to talk to your child about how the magazines make her feel when she reads them. If she says they cheer her up, then you may consider leaving them. But, if they make her have negative thoughts about her own body (as is the case for many young women) or believe that being excessively thin is the only way to be attractive, then you can ask her what she thinks about putting the magazines away for a short time. You can treat this as an experiment where the magazines are put away for two weeks, and then you can check to see how your daughter feels without them. In this way, you can talk to your daughter about her thoughts and feelings on this matter and decide together whether or not to have these magazines in the house.

An alternative strategy is to replace the popular, old-fashioned magazines with new, more positive ones. Two examples are *O Magazine* and *Grace Mazagine*, which do not include such unhealthy images. These magazines show a range of body shapes and aspire to challenge negative societal images of waif-thin women. It can also be helpful to tell your daughter about the "truth" behind fashion magazines—that even models like Cindy Crawford do not look like their pictures in real life! The bodies that appear in print have been retouched using computer graphics, often to make the model appear even skinnier than she is in reality.

Question: "I have struggled with my weight my whole life. I know I have said things like 'I feel so fat' in front of my daughter, but that is how I really feel! Am I supposed to censor everything I say?"

Answer: There is a phenomenon among women in our society that has been termed "fat talk." There is even a book by the same name that critiques what girls say about their bodies and dieting and what role that seems to be playing in how females relate to each other (Nichter 2000). Essentially, it has become the norm for women and girls to talk about feeling fat, sometimes because they really are overweight and other times because they just want to join in this type of conversation with other women. We suggest that you fight this tendency in yourself and your household, and try to avoid saying that you feel fat in front of your child. You can say that you are concerned about your health, or that you feel frustrated because you cannot engage in certain activities due to your weight (if this is true). However, it is likely that no matter what your weight, you can work toward greater physical fitness, which is an important predictor of good health (Blair and Brodney 1999) and a healthy behavior to model for your children.

Question: "I am overweight and am on a diet. Should I hide this from my child?"

Answer: There is nothing wrong with working to improve your health, and this is a great goal to model for your child as long as you do it in a healthy, reasonable way. You can talk about your efforts to improve your health through eating balanced meals and, as you lose weight, expressing that you feel better now that you can do more physical things, like riding your bike with your kids or hiking with the family. We suggest that you avoid saying that you are excited to fit into a particular clothing size or emphasizing the changes in your appearance, because this may send the message to your child that the main reason to lose weight is to look better, instead of to improve your health.

Shoshana's Story

Shoshana was a seventeen-year-old high school senior when she began restricting her food intake. She had always been a little bit overweight, but she was an excellent student and enjoyed many sports. She had never had a boyfriend and felt in awe of the girls in her school who were already dating. She was in the midst of filling out college applications when she began to panic about leaving home and moving away to a new school. Shoshana knew her parents were really proud of her grades and expected her to get into a very competitive school. Both of her parents were college professors and felt that nothing was more important than a good education. Shoshana was worried that she would not be accepted at her top choice school and she could not imagine disappointing her parents. She felt that if she did not get into the best school on her list, she might as well not go to college at all. Shoshana had never been very good at talking about her feelings and usually just tried to do what her parents and teachers wanted her to do, because that way everyone was happy.

As she filled out her applications, she also thought a lot about her social life. She'd been going to school with the same kids since kindergarten, which meant that everyone knew her quite well. However, she also felt that she couldn't become part of the popular crowd because she already had her group of friends. She began to imagine losing twenty pounds and becoming a new person. In college, she could reinvent herself and become thin, glamorous, and popular. She began restricting her food intake by not eating desserts or breads, and lost a few pounds quickly. Others noticed and told her how great she looked, and this made her feel like she should continue to lose weight. She kept restricting her food intake, but it seemed that the more she did it, the more rules she had to develop. At first, she eliminated snacks and desserts, and then she stopped eating anything with butter, salt, sauces, and gravy. After that, she added to her list of food rules by reducing the amount of carbohydrates she ate, and she eventually cut all carbs out of her diet. She knew that her parents would not like what she was doing, so she hid her behaviors from them as much as she could.

As her weight continued to drop, her parents noticed and became very concerned. Shoshana's mother had a sister who had suffered from anorexia nervosa, so she recognized the symptoms in her daughter. The family sought therapy and tried to identify the factors that had placed Shoshana at risk for developing anorexia nervosa. They learned that Shoshana may have inherited genetic factors from her maternal side of the family that put her at risk. They also learned that several aspects of Shoshana's personality, such as a tendency toward perfectionism and all-or-nothing thinking, may have been maintaining the disorder. In addition, preparing to leave home and go to college may have been a contributing stressful life event. Finally, Shoshana's difficulty identifying and discussing her negative feelings with others left her with few other ways of coping with her anxiety.

Julia's Story

Julia was a twenty-year-old college sophomore when she and her sorority sisters decided to go on a diet and lose some weight. They began by making vegetarian meals together and encouraging each other to exercise each day. Everyone lost a few pounds, but then the others decided it was too much work and went back to their old ways of eating.

In contrast, Julia found it hard to go back to her old eating habits. She liked not eating meat, so she decided to remain a vegetarian. She found that when she got on the scale each morning and saw that she had lost weight, she felt a great sense of accomplishment. Losing weight became the focus of her day. She would wake up and weigh herself, and then go running and weigh herself again. Sometimes, she would even weigh herself after she went to the bathroom to see if her weight had changed.

Julia decided that she not only wanted to eliminate meat from her diet but other animal products too, like dairy products. She told others it was because she didn't like the idea of eating things that came from animals, but she knew inside that the real reason was that cheese and milk had fat in them. Meanwhile, she increasingly limited what she could eat and started to refuse social invitations involving food because she felt like everyone would stare at her plate and think she was a pig.

When she went home for winter break, her parents were shocked to see her and took her immediately to the doctor. The doctor diagnosed her with anorexia nervosa and referred her to a specialty clinic for eating disorders. During the initial evaluation, one of the questions asked was whether or not she had ever experienced trauma. Until then, Julia had never told anyone that she had been date raped during the fall semester, right before her "diet" began. She was embarrassed and thought that it was her fault because she was drunk at the time. She felt that she could have tried harder to fight off the boy.

In therapy, she learned that the rape was not her fault, and she gained insight into the ways in which restricting her food had made her feel as if she had control over the traumatic experience. Julia and her family met a few times to discuss what had been going on for her during the semester, and she continued to make progress in regaining weight and restoring her eating to healthy levels. While receiving treatment for her eating disorder, Julia participated in a therapy group for survivors of sexual trauma to talk about her fears and guilt following the rape.

Creating Solutions

In this chapter, we have discussed many of the potential risk factors that may contribute to the development of an eating disorder. Each individual has his or her own genetic makeup, family patterns, and personal history that may have promoted disordered eating. Now would be a good time to think about what factors may have led to your child's eating difficulties. Here are some questions to get you started:

- How much does your family watch TV, read magazines, or see popular movies?

- Do you find that you compare yourself to actresses or models you see in ads?

- How often do people in your family engage in "fat talk" where you discuss feeling fat or questioning whether certain clothes make you look fat?

- What is your child's weight history. Were there times she or he was overweight? Underweight?

- Have there been specific traumatic events that have occurred in your family (such as the death of a family member, loss of a home, parental divorce, parental loss of a job)?

- Do members of your family talk about negative emotions, such as fear, disappointment, and anger? How are these feelings handled at home?

- Does your child participate in extracurricular activities that emphasize weight, like wrestling, ballet, or gymnastics?

These questions serve to highlight possible issues and risk factors that can make your child more or less vulnerable to having an eating disorder. It is not always possible to pinpoint one key event or cause. Sometimes specific, seemingly unimportant events can trigger the actual onset of an eating disorder. Consider these examples:

- Has your child recently had a disappointing experience (such as difficulty with a subject at school or poor performance at a sporting event)?

- Has your child changed friends or broken up with a boyfriend or girlfriend?

- Is your child in the midst of a transition from one school to another (for example, leaving middle school and entering high school, or graduating from high school or college)?

In thinking about what attitudes you and your family have about eating and body image, it is sometimes useful to think back to your own childhood:

- Do you remember either of your parents or siblings struggling with food?

- Do others in your extended families have difficulties with weight?

- What comments did you hear while growing up about your body and eating habits?

- Did you or your partner go on diets as children?

Do not feel frustrated if the range of possible causes of eating disorders overwhelms you. This is a natural response, but you can tie the pieces together. The following list of categories reflects the main contributing causes of eating disorders. Write down your ideas about what factors may have played, or currently play, a role in the development or maintenance of your child's eating problems:

Society:_____

_____

_____

Life events:_____

_____

_____

Individual factors: _____

_____

_____

Negative influences from family and friends:_____

_____

_____

Unhealthy eating patterns: _____

_____

_____

Self-defeating thoughts: _____

_____

_____

Biological factors: _____

_____

_____

This list can be used as a starting point for opening discussions with your child. It can also aid your child's therapist in understanding the complex history of your child's difficulties with eating. Remember that gaining insight into the causes of eating disorders should not be a reason for guilt, but can be a helpful step toward formulating the solutions needed for your family.

CHAPTER 4

What Do You Say?
Family Communication and Eating Disorders

Yesterday when Molly got home from school, she came into the house, dropped her coat on the table, and headed for the stairs. I said, "Hi, honey. How was your day?" "Fine," she said, without turning around. "Wait up, Molly, I want to talk to you about something." "I can't right now, Mom, I have too much homework." I heard her door close. I can't even get her attention long enough to talk about the weather—how am I supposed to talk to her about her eating disorder?

—Charlotte, mother of a sixteen-year-old girl with bulimia nervosa

Talking to adolescents can be difficult under the best of circumstances. In the case of a family where a teenager has an eating disorder, things can be even more complicated. It can be very difficult to figure out which of your child's behaviors are "normal" adolescent developmental issues and which are symptoms of a more serious problem.

Parenting is one of life's most challenging jobs. Part of what makes it so hard is that the job description is constantly changing. Just when you think you know how to talk to your child, things change. Parents report that their children used to talk about school and friends, but that as their children enter adolescence, they stop sharing so much with them. To some degree, it is normal for children to begin to rely on their peers for support and information, but do not think that means that you do not matter. What you say and do does matter.

In this chapter, we discuss the issue of family communication and provide concrete strategies for you to try at home. We consider common myths about communicating with young people about eating disorders and outline techniques to help you speak with your child and other family members about a range of issues related to eating, shape, and weight. Next, we discuss how to plan family meetings and determine the appropriate structure and discipline that you should provide to best support ongoing family communication about these difficult issues. As always, we respond to common questions we hear from families about communication, provide illustrative case examples, and help you to create solutions that are right for you and your family.

Debunking Myths about Family Communication

Myth: My child never listens to me anyway, so it really doesn't matter what I say.

Research says: What you say and do has a huge impact on your child's life. While it may not feel like it, you are still an important part of your child's life during this time. Research shows that your personality and values as a parent create an environment that is unique to your family and helps to shape who your children are and who they will become.

Although it can be frustrating, your child is actually going through a normal part of growing up and becoming a young adult by distancing her- or himself from you. Adolescence is a time when children begin to break away from their parents and establish their own independence and identity. Part of this means making their own decisions and figuring out their own interests and beliefs apart from yours. This is a healthy process and does not mean that you no longer play an important role in your child's life. In fact, even during adolescence, most children still turn to their parents for guidance and support.

Research indicates that your relationship with your children influences the way they see themselves. For example, relationships that are supportive and affectionate let children know that they are loved and accepted. On the other hand, relationships that are unemotional, closed, or more reserved may communicate to children that you do not understand their needs or that you feel their problems are not legitimate. It's important for you to find ways to show your child that you care!

Myth: If you feel uncomfortable talking about something, then it's better just to ignore the subject or you'll make things worse.

Research says: Keeping your thoughts and feelings to yourself can negatively affect your relationship with your child. Some researchers speculate that when you hold back your feelings, your mind has to work that much harder to keep those thoughts hidden. The added mental stress that you experience when you keep your feelings to yourself puts a very real physical strain on your body (Pennebaker 1989). This strain can weaken your immune system (Pennebaker, Kiecolt-Glaser, and Glaser 1989) and result in a number of other physical illnesses.

Not talking about something that makes you uncomfortable and uneasy can also affect your relationship with your child and can complicate things later on. No matter how hard you try to hide your feelings, they usually end up coming out in other ways. As a result, without realizing it, you may become frustrated or anxious around your child, your tone of voice and body language may become different, or you may find yourself set off by little things—reactions that could make your child feel more confused and defensive since she or he will probably not understand why you are acting this way. By expressing yourself to your child and other family members, you let your child know that it is all right to be honest and open. At the same time you are communicating to your child that you accept and are ready to learn about all of him or her—not only the positive and easygoing aspects of your child's life and personality, but also the more complex, sad, angry, and difficult sides.

Myth: The way a person thinks or talks can't change. That's just how it is.

Research says: Change is possible, and treatment can help make it happen—but sometimes your child may need a little push from you to get there. The good news is that people with eating disorders can and do change, and therapy is often one of the key ingredients in this process. People who enter into treatment have much better chances for recovery than those who do not. The help and guidance of a professional can be useful for learning how to change effectively and on a long-term basis.

The hard part in all of this is recognizing when to let your child make the decision to start treatment and when to step in as a parent and make the decision yourself. Sometimes it is possible for you or a therapist to motivate your child for treatment by eliciting his or her own concerns about the eating disorder and desire for change (Tober 1991). Other situations may require treatment at your insistence before your child feels ready to do so. This is especially true if your child's disorder has become dangerous or life-threatening—for example, if body weight is drastically low or harmful medical consequences are occurring (Lock, et al. 2001). In these circumstances, taking your child to a therapist may help to get things started; other cases may require involuntary hospitalization.

Once your child is in treatment, it is important to realize that the condition may not improve right away. People change at their own pace. At different points in your child's illness, he or she may be more or less ready to commit to change. No matter how frustrated and discouraged you may feel, it is important not to give up hope. Families who work hard in therapy and have faith in their child getting better will likely experience more positive treatment outcomes later on.

Talking about Eating, Shape, and Weight

Talking about an issue as painful as your child's eating disorder is extremely difficult for most parents. It is also unlikely that your child will feel comfortable initially, so it can feel tempting to avoid the subject and just hope it will go away. However, in the long run it is usually better to confront the issues and negative feelings. Don't be afraid to express anger, confusion, or frustration. Doing so can lead to more open communication. Distancing yourself from the problem, pretending nothing has happened, or making light of the situation rarely improve difficulties or make you feel closer to your child. Regardless of whether your child wants to talk about the problem, it is important for you to have an outlet to discuss your own feelings and concerns.

You may feel that you are being compassionate when you repeatedly reassure your child that he or she is not fat. However, it is unlikely that your child will believe you, given that people with eating disorders have distorted impressions of their appearance. In addition, repeatedly providing reassurance can set up a vicious cycle, where your child asks you over and over again if he or she looks okay. This cycle is problematic because your child is relying on you to establish his or her self-esteem instead of learning to feel good based on his or her own judgment. It can also feel very frustrating especially if your child disagrees with your reassurance.

Instead of trying to convince your child that her or his weight is fine and should not be such a concern, you will probably be more successful if you talk about the eating disorder directly. Researchers have developed the "IMAD" approach to guide people in talking to their loved ones about their illness (Levine and Hill 1991). They recommend that you focus on the inefficiency, misery, alienation, and disturbance (IMAD) that the illness is causing in your child's life. The idea is not to make your child feel attacked or ashamed, but to be open about the problem and talk about its impact in a straightforward way.

Inefficiency is a term you can use when discussing how the eating disorder prevents your child from accomplishing things. For example, what are the consequences of the physical weakness that follows from either restricted eating or purging behaviors? What are the effects of sadness, anxiety, low energy, and poor concentration? What about the impact of the time spent on the eating disorder, such as time spent finding binge foods, excessively exercising, or hiding the vomiting and other behaviors? You can talk with your child about how these factors interfere with relationships with friends and family, school life, social activities and other personal goals.

Misery sums up the emotional consequences of an eating disorder. You and your child can talk about the times she or he feels anger, depression, anxiety, guilt, or other negative emotions. How often are these painful feelings related to the eating disorder in some way (such as feeling ashamed after throwing up, guilty after eating, depressed because of feeling fat and alone)?

Alienation may occur because the constant obsession with eating, weight, exercise, and body image leads to social isolation and the feeling that no one really knows or understands you. The resulting sense of loneliness can be very overwhelming. You can talk with your child about ways he or she has become cut off from you, other family members and friends. Also, you can help your child to think about how he or she might even feel cut off from him- or herself.

Disturbance is a term you can use to talk about behaviors the person is doing that are frightening or generally upsetting to either himself or to others. For example, people often find it disturbing that they feel the need to eat in secret, hoard food, take laxatives, weigh themselves repeatedly, or vomit. Moodiness and irritability associated with eating disorders is another common source of disturbance, along with impulsive behaviors such as lying, being promiscuous or stealing food or money.

These are very sensitive issues, and discussing them may feel uncomfortable at first for both you and your child. We have included some ideas to help you prepare and to make the conversations flow a little more smoothly.

Make a Plan to Talk with Your Child

Choose a quiet time to talk when you will have some privacy and will not feel rushed. Write down when and where you will have this talk. Set a date, time, and location.

It's important to be open and honest about your concerns. Use concrete examples to help your child see that the problem is real and that you care and worry about his or her health, happiness, and safety. Identify your concerns. Here are some examples:

- "I've noticed that you do not eat with the family."

- "It worries me that you do not seem happy."

- "I have noticed that you do not go out with friends anymore."

Write down some of the concerns that you plan to express:

_____

_____

_____

When you express these concerns, it is important to avoid sounding like you are placing blame or guilt on your child for these behaviors. Your child probably feels guilty and ashamed already, and giving the impression that you are accusing your child or think that she or he has failed will only add to your child's strain and feelings of alienation. So, instead of making accusatory statements, such as "You just need to stop vomiting" or "You are messing up your life," try to avoid phrases that start with "you." Instead, express your concerns from the standpoint of what you see and feel by using the word "I." For example, try replacing the phrase "you don't eat enough" with "I am really concerned that eating so little is hurting your health." Try rewriting the "you" statements below into more supportive "I" sentences.

"You" accusations	"I" support statements
"You let me down."	_____
"You steal food from the fridge."	_____
"You look too skinny."	_____
"You are setting a bad example for your siblings."	_____
"You make a mess of the bathroom when you vomit."	_____
"You left an empty box of laxatives in the bathroom."	_____
"You should know better than this."	_____
"What's wrong with you?"	_____

Keep in mind that there are many ways to transform a "you" statement into an "I" statement, depending on your particular circumstances and communication style. We've come up with some ideas for the previous statements. If your statements aren't exactly like the ideas we've provided, it doesn't mean that yours are wrong—instead, you might find a few more ways to rephrase your concerns. Here are some examples:

1. "I'm disappointed about what's happened."

2. "Food has been missing from the refrigerator, and I'm worried that you've been eating it."

3. "I'm concerned about your health."

4. "The whole family is affected by our difficulties, and I'm worried about your brothers and sisters."

5. "I've noticed that there's often a mess in the bathroom, and I'd like for us to talk about this. We need to come up with a plan so that vomit isn't left in or on the toilet."

6. "I found an empty box of laxatives in the bathroom; I need to talk with you about this."

7. "I'm so worried about you, and I feel like I don't know what to do to help you."

8. "I don't understand why you're bingeing and purging. I'd like to help. Let's talk about seeing a professional for an evaluation."

Make it clear that you love and care for your child but are very concerned about his or her health. Talk to your child about the value of seeing a professional for an evaluation. The idea of seeing a therapist is likely to alarm your child, so find out what his or her concerns are. Point out that many people need help at some point in their lives. It is the people who admit to problems and try to solve them who are brave, not the people who deny that they are struggling and never get better.

- Explain that you will help to find someone your child feels comfortable talking to, and you will accompany your child to the appointment if that would help.

- Let your child know that recovery is *much* easier if you deal with the eating disorder earlier, rather than later.

- Try not to scare your child, but let him or her know the very severe medical and psychological consequences of eating disorders that can occur if left untreated.

- Tell your child that seeing a therapist does not mean that he or she is crazy—it just means that with this illness he or she needs special care.

- Remind your child that many people suffer with these problems, and effective treatments are available that can lead to a happier life.

Your child may be resistant to these ideas at first, but do not give up hope. Try to avoid arguing, but be firm about your concerns and let your child know that you are available to talk or help whenever he or she feels ready. Give your child some time to absorb the conversation, then raise your concerns again at another time. At the end of every conversation, remind your child that you love him or her, feel concerned, and want to help.

How to Talk about Body Image and Health

One of the most helpful things you can do as a parent is to speak with your family about healthy ways to think about shape, weight, and dieting. These discussions are critical not only for the child with the eating problem but also for other family members. You can raise thought-provoking topics to discuss together in an effort to help your family be more aware of their own thoughts and behaviors and the role that our culture plays in promoting beauty myths about thinness. In addition, you can work together to change the language your family uses to talk about their own and each other's bodies and eating.

We suggest that you find a quiet time to raise these issues when there is not a lot of tension or negative feelings in the house, because these topics can be sensitive and emotional. Do not be discouraged if your family is not immediately responsive—keep trying. The idea is to encourage discussion and new ideas, not to be accusatory or blaming or even to pretend that there are simple solutions to these complex problems. The following topics are not listed in any order, so you can choose whatever feels most meaningful to you and seems most age-appropriate for your children.

Topics for Family Discussions

- Why do people (women in particular) tend to be so negative about their own bodies? What is the impact on our self-esteem and relationships, and why does our society value physical appearance and thinness so much?

- Why is it that even young girls feel pressured to diet when they have healthy, growing bodies? What role might toys like Barbie dolls (that present an entirely unrealistic body shape) play in our desperate struggle to be thin? Let your children know that a woman shaped like Barbie could not survive; her waist is so small compared to her chest that her ribs would collapse!

- Think about the way you talk about your own body. Why is it that we rarely think about the fact that our bodies need food for fuel, and that it is because of this energy that our bodies do so many amazing things for us, like run and climb stairs?

- In the real world, bodies come in all shapes and sizes, but on TV we rarely see people who are not slim. Moreover, when obese people are portrayed in the media, they are often the victims of "fat jokes" or other forms of discrimination. Use this point to help your children recognize the nature and ugliness of prejudice.

- Talk about the large role that genetics and the environment play in determining our body shape, and discuss how all of us have a natural set weight at which our body is healthy and comfortable. Let your child know the dangers of trying to get below this weight through extreme dieting. Think about whether life would really be all that different if you were ten pounds lighter or heavier, and question whether the lengths people go to with fad diets, pills, and plastic surgery are really worth it.

Re-creating Language

Often people have great intentions to change their thoughts and behaviors about food and weight but do not know where to begin. You can start by becoming aware of the negative language you use and trying to use supportive statements instead of critical ones. We have put together a list of some common insults we hear people using against themselves and others, and we offer some alternatives that are more positive and kind. See if you can recognize the negative comments that you inadvertently make, and try to generate more healthy statements that reflect a healthier attitude toward eating and body shape. Here are some examples of unhealthy language about body shape:

- "I am fat."

- "I am a pig."

- "You have thunder thighs."

- "That dress would look better on you if you lost five pounds."

- "You're never going to get a date if you don't lose weight."

- "Guys only like skinny girls."

- "My stomach is huge."

- "I look like a whale."

Do you make similar statements? What are they?

_____

_____

_____

_____

Here are some examples of healthy alternatives:

- "I am healthy."

- "I am strong."

- "You look good just the way you are."

- "People of all shapes and sizes are attractive."

- "What I am like on the inside is what really matters."

- "I deserve to feel good about myself."

- "I take care of and respect my body."

- "Having a belly is natural for women."

- "I like that I have curves."

- "There are lots of clothes that look good on me."

Add some positive statements of your own.

_____

_____

_____

_____

Here are some examples of unhealthy language about food and eating:

- "I shouldn't have this cake."

- "God, you eat a lot."

- "I am never going to eat potato chips."

- "Chocolate is bad for you."

- "I can only have the ice cream if I've been good today."

- "If I eat this tonight, I have to go back on my diet tomorrow."

- "I'm being good and just having salad."

- "You don't look like you need any dessert."

Do you make negative statements about food and eating? What are they?

_____

_____

_____

_____

Here are healthy alternatives:

- "I need food to be healthy."

- "Food gives my body energy."

- "I want to enjoy this dessert and not feel guilty."

- "Food tastes good. I shouldn't be afraid of it."

- "I can eat all different kinds of food as long as I eat them in moderation."

- "I am going to eat regularly and not skip meals."

- "If I am hungry, I will let myself eat."

- "Eating this ice cream doesn't make me a bad person."

- "I am not going to eat in secret because I have nothing to be ashamed of."

- "It's okay to feel like my stomach isn't empty."

Your ideas:

_____

_____

_____

_____

Talking with Your Family

Every family has its own style of interacting, and you are probably already doing lots of positive things to encourage communication within your family. Learning new ways of talking with each other can be very intimidating, but it can also be an important part of the recovery process. We hope that the following general guidelines will be useful to you in evaluating and improving how the members of your family communicate:

1. Establish open and honest communication from the outset. There is a lot of shame and secrecy associated with eating disorders, so you want to create a warm environment that makes your child feel safe to share his or her feelings with you.

2. Remember that everyone in the family is struggling with the impact of this disorder. Always ask yourself how your family can best move forward in this situation, rather than ruminate about the past. Try not to be punishing or blaming.

3. Consider the needs of all family members. Make sure that you, your partner, and all of your children are not being neglected.

4. Set up clear expectations in advance so that you do not make faulty assumptions or get caught up in the heat of the moment. This includes planning who will take responsibility for chores and determining the consequences for disruptive behaviors before they take place.

Remember that you are setting an example for the rest of your family; think about the messages you send through your behavior and your reactions to emotional situations. Your children should know that your love for them is not conditional. Be consistent in the enforcement of guidelines so that you do not send mixed messages. However, keep in mind that the consequences for misbehaving should be fair and age appropriate, so you may need to establish different plans for children of different ages. Once you have enforced a consequence, try not to hold a grudge or dwell on the situation after it is over. Do not hesitate to contact a therapist or friend when you have a question—remember that you are not alone in this!

Family involvement is strongly recommended and at times required when a young person has an eating disorder, and many families benefit from parent counseling and family therapy. The goal of these types of support is to help your family to function more effectively, not to blame anyone. While there are many approaches to working with families, a common element is the importance of the "4Cs" (Lask and Bryant-Waugh, 1997). These may be helpful for you to consider as you think about how your family operates:

Cohesion. Parents need to work effectively together, so that family members are not given mixed messages.

Consistency. Consistency across time is important. Of course, some of your family rules will change as the recovery process progresses and as your child's developmental needs change, but consistency in your rules from day to day limits confusion, which can be helpful to all family members.

Communication. Again, we cannot overstress the importance of clear, open communication that allows all family members a chance to speak for themselves.

Conflict resolution. Finding healthy ways to resolve conflict as a family is central to strong family functioning. You need to be able to hear opposing viewpoints and learn how to disagree with each other.

Establish Regular Family Meetings

Regular family meetings allow all members of the family to express their questions and concerns, in order to solve problems and prevent new difficulties. We recommend that you hold meetings approximately every two weeks and that all family members be encouraged to attend (unless you are concerned that very young siblings would not be emotionally mature enough for the subject matter). Once you get in the habit of holding these meetings, they will take on a structure of their own, but planning the first meeting can be intimidating. We suggest that you hold the meetings at a time other than during meals and in a place that feels safe for everyone (for example, not in the kitchen, but perhaps in the living room).

Emphasize honest and open communication at these meetings and do not reject anyone's ideas or feelings. Direct communication usually works most effectively, so do not hesitate to ask clear questions, such as, "Where should junk food be kept in the house so that you do not feel tempted to binge?" Direct questions provide the best opportunity for clear answers and minimize misunderstandings.

Do not be disappointed if all family members do not speak up or voice concerns initially—it takes a while to learn how to communicate openly. Simply be patient and continue to demonstrate respect for all viewpoints. At all costs, you want to avoid turning these meetings into a screaming match, so if the discussion becomes combative, it may be necessary to take a break and try again at another time. Explain to all family members that the goal is compromise, so that the entire family can feel good about the established living arrangements. The purpose is not to give special attention to the child with the eating disorder; all family members have needs and are equally important members of the household.

Coping with Disagreement

Some families find that, while most members agree to participate in family meetings, one parent or child may say he or she does not want to attend. In this case, we encourage you to go ahead and hold the meeting, rather than force him or her to be involved. You do not want to add to the tension and negative feelings in the household, and pressuring someone to participate is unlikely to result in a positive environment. If certain family members do not want to attend, we suggest that you ask why. Sometimes people fear they will be blamed for a sibling's eating disorder or fear that these meetings will result in privileges being taken away. If this is the case, you can use this opportunity to allay their fears.

If they still feel uncomfortable joining in, you can let them know what happens at the meetings so that they do not feel left out. Given that they will have to abide by the rules determined at the meetings they may be more open to participating once it becomes clear that, by attending meetings, they can actually play a role in formulating these rules.

The goal is to make the meetings a positive experience and to always keep the door open so that family members who are initially hesitant can change their minds and join in as their comfort level increases. Try not to be discouraged by initial resistance. It is not unusual for siblings of ill family members to react in a wide variety of positive and negative ways, sometimes with tolerance, insight, and compassion while at other times becoming aggressive or withdrawing. Time, understanding, and support can help individuals adjust to the new challenges facing the family.

So far, our suggestions have assumed that all family members live in one household. If you are separated or divorced, and the children spend time at more than one house, you will need to communicate the outcomes of these meetings to the other parent. Research suggests that it is important for you to provide as consistent an environment for your child as possible. Children who perceive inconsistencies in parenting can be at risk for lowered self-esteem and other negative outcomes (Johnson, Shulman, and Collins 1991).

The Unique Role of Parents

For as long as there have been parents, there have been people who think they know the best way to do the job of parenting! As we said earlier, parenting is probably the hardest job anyone will ever have. The responsibility of taking a newborn baby home and being completely in charge of his or her survival is awe-inspiring. Despite this, there are no clear guidelines for how to do this job. There are certainly books written by experts who are more than willing to give their opinions, but if you review these books, you will probably find just as many opinions as there are experts.

Parenting Styles

We do not want to presume to know the right way for you to parent your family, but we do want to help you think through different choices. This way, you can find a solution that works for your personality and your family. The most popular research on being a mother or father divides parenting styles into four general types that display different degrees of warmth and control (Baumrind 1991). These four types are: authoritarian, authoritative, indulgent and neglectful. These terms may sound complicated, but they are types of parenting you will probably recognize pretty easily:

Authoritarian parents try to control their children and are not very warm (low warmth, high control). They have very high expectations of what children are supposed to do and focus on trying to get their children to obey them. For example, they will use harsh punishment to get their children to cooperate. As a result of this type of parenting, children may become high achievers and do well academically, but they also tend to have difficulties socially and feel bad about themselves (Baumrind 1991; Steinberg, et al. 1994).

Authoritative parents work to combine control with warmth (moderate warmth and control). They set clear rules and have high standards for their children, but they also explain the rationale for their decisions. Parents of this type tend to have a lot of family discussions. They encourage independence in their children, who are usually more responsible, reliable, and psychologically healthy. Children who grow up in homes where parents have an authoritative style often do well in school, have good social skills, and experience few psychological and behavioral problems (Baumrind 1991; Steinberg, et al. 1994).

Indulgent parents are very warm and caring but demonstrate very little influence or control with their children (high warmth, low control). They tend to make few demands on their children and do not set up rules or consequences for breaking rules. This style of parenting often results in children who do fairly well socially and enjoy their peers but are also inclined toward behavior problems in addition to not doing well in school (Baumrind 1991; Steinberg, et al. 1994).

Neglectful parents show little control and warmth to their children (low warmth, low control). Basically, they try to minimize the amount of time they spend with their children and do not put much effort into parenting. Children of these parents often exhibit serious behavior problems and do poorly in school (Baumrind 1991; Steinberg, et al. 1994).

Most parents do not fall neatly in any of these categories, but display different styles at various times. For example, parents may try to be authoritative but, when it comes time for their child to apply to colleges, they might use authoritarian strategies to get their child to focus on filling out the applications. When these same parents are completely stressed with work-related issues, they may seem more like neglectful parents. In other cases, where one parent has an authoritarian style, the other parent may find him or herself using a more permissive style to balance things out.

What Is Your Style?

To help you think about your style as a parent, spend a few moments thinking about the variety of ways that you and your child relate to each other, including positive, negative, and neutral experiences. Consider times when you've disagreed and times when you've had to impose consequences for unacceptable behavior. Also reflect on your day-to-day interactions with your child, as well as fun times together. Use the spaces below to write down two or three recent experiences that come to mind:

_____

_____

_____

_____

_____

Now, in each of these situations, think about yourself from your child's perspective: How does he or she experience you? How would he or she describe you? Come up with examples of when your child would have experienced you in the following ways:

Warm _____

_____

Caring_____

_____

Having clear rules_____

_____

Involved_____

_____

Interested _____

_____

Open _____

_____

Honest _____

_____

What are some other ways your child might describe you?

_____

_____

_____

Given that the research is clear about the advantages of having an authoritative parenting style, what changes can you make to more closely resemble this style? How can you improve the ways in which you relate to your child? Are there times when you can express more warmth, show more interest, be more involved, have clearer rules, be more understanding, promote more independence? List some changes you would like to make:

_____

_____

_____

_____

The purpose of discussing these styles is not to make you look back and see all of the times you were not the best parent that you could have been. Instead, this is an opportunity to think about your parenting strategies and to find new strategies that will help you in the challenges you face as a family.

When to Intervene

Many parents find it difficult to decide which of their child's behaviors they should try to change and which they should leave alone. Here are some questions that you can consider as you evaluate each new situation:

- Is this behavior life threatening?

- Should you try to help?

- Should you put aside your own needs?

Is This Behavior Life Threatening?

If the behavior is life threatening, then it is your job as a parent to try to exert some influence. How exactly you do this will depend on the specific needs of your child and situation in your family, but we urge you to get professional advice if you are in any of these positions:

- If your child is starving him or herself, it is important to try to work with a professional team to help your child resume normal eating.

- If your child threatens suicide or threatens to harm someone else, take this seriously by getting help such as by calling 911.

- If your child has been vomiting or using laxatives, talk about what you've observed and encourage your child to meet with a healthcare professional.

When your child's behaviors are not life threatening, deciding how to proceed can be very tricky. Many parents disapprove of their children's behaviors in domains that are not a matter of life and death. For example, you may be frustrated with your child because she refuses to practice the piano even though she has a recital coming up. You are worried she will be embarrassed (and perhaps that you will be embarrassed as well) when she doesn't perform well. While this is certainly not desirable, it is not a matter of life and death. At times, it may make sense to allow your child to learn the consequences of her choices on her own. We are not suggesting that you only intervene on life and death issues but that you consider the importance of a contentious issue, so you can effectively "pick your battles."

Should You Try to Help?

There are no easy answers to this question. Every family is unique and each child has different needs; however, as a general rule of thumb, you can do the following when dealing with problems that are not life threatening:

1. Talk to your child about what you've observed. You can say for example: "I'm concerned because I've noticed that you haven't been practicing for your gymnastics meet."

2. Offer to help. You can say: "I'm here to talk about it if that would help," or "Let me know what I can do to help."

If your child refuses your help, you might not be able to do much to change the situation. It will be important for you to assess the problem and consider if continued attempts at intervention will improve things or make matters worse. There are times when backing away from the problem after expressing your concern might be the best option. Here are some questions to consider when thinking about how to proceed:

- If you have already expressed concern and offered to help, what else can you do to help?

- What are the possible consequences of trying to intervene again? (Consider your child's position and your own frustration level, as well as the likelihood of a positive final outcome.)

- What are the possible consequences of not intervening again? (Consider your child's position, your own frustration level, as well as the likelihood of a positive final outcome.)

Should You Put Aside Your Own Needs?

When a child is ill, it is easy to feel both that you should be doing everything you can to help and resentful that so much of your time is being spent taking care of someone else. These are normal feelings. We urge you to seek help for yourself at this time as well. You will be a better parent if you feel like your own needs are being taken care of as well as your child's.

As each situation comes up, try to make a decision based on appropriate expectations for your child and yourself. If your child's health is in danger, then you need to intervene. If it is not, then you may choose to stay out of it. When you want to help your child with something, explain what you are willing to do and when, and then let your child decide whether or not to take you up on your offer. If she or he does not accept your help, do not feel like you need to bend over backwards later on. The key is to be clear in communicating this to your child ahead of time. If you have done this, you can feel confident that you have been fair and explained your behaviors in a clear and consistent manner.

Questions and Answers about Family Communication

Question: "I've heard that if I ask my daughter a lot of questions about her eating problems, it can make things worse or even give her ideas about new ways to hurt herself. So, should I bring up my concerns or just stay quiet?"

Answer: Although talking about the eating disorder is a scary proposition, keep in mind that your daughter is aware of the problem and suffering because of it, regardless of whether or not you talk about it openly. Research suggests that it can be much healthier to deal with conflict in a direct and supportive way, rather than to ignore the problem. In fact, there is a tendency for families of children with eating disorders to avoid conflict (Vandereycken 2002), which is understandable given how painful disagreements can be, but it may not be helpful in the long run. Secrecy and hiding frustration can set families up for more conflict in the future. Family members are often left to guess what is upsetting the other person, which can easily lead to misunderstandings and hurt feelings.

When children do not express their negative emotions, it seems the most common reason is fear of a negative reaction from others (Zeman and Garber 1996). This suggests to us that you can best help your child by creating an open environment where people can express their feelings without fear. This does not mean that every negative feeling or comment should be endorsed, but the challenge is for all family members to respect one another's opinions and feelings so that issues can be addressed directly in a collaborative way.

Question: "How do I relate to my child now?"

Answer: The goal here is to strike a balance between promoting your child's independence and providing her with structure and guidance. Tasks that may have once been easy for your child can now seem overwhelming as she tries to cope with the eating disorder. Thus, she may need help in areas in which she had previously been fully independent. You want her to feel that she has your support when she needs it; however, you want to encourage her to live as normally and independently as possible.

Along these lines, we recommend experimenting with different levels of independence and responsibility until both you and your child feel comfortable. For example, your child may wish to have full control over her weekend plans, so you and she may decide to try this option for a period of three weeks. However, if you find that she is retreating to her bedroom during this time, you may want to renegotiate and take a more active role in helping her structure activities. This will need to be an ongoing negotiation, as she will become able to take on more responsibility throughout the recovery process.

Question: "What should we do if we find out that our child is engaging in harmful behaviors and not telling us about them?"

Answer: We recommend that you discuss this issue as early as possible and establish a contract. For example, you may decide that if you discover an unhealthy, secretive behavior, you will first tell your child that you are worried about him, then explain that you feel it is necessary to tell a therapist or other professional. Be very clear from the outset that the goal is not to talk about him behind his back, but to make sure he gets the help he needs. Along these lines, we do not encourage parents to "snoop" around for evidence of possible harmful behaviors (for example, looking through drawers for laxatives). This does not encourage open communication and may set up barriers between you and your child, preventing you from providing him with the support that he needs. Instead, you can articulate your observations about your child's behavior and express your concerns about his welfare.

We recognize that having this kind of conversation is difficult and you may fear that your child will turn away from you. However, expressing your concerns and not avoiding conflict promotes healthy open communication in the family.

Question: "What do we do when our child asks us how she looks, or if we think she's fat?"

Answer: This issue arises frequently. It is important to recognize that individuals with an eating disorder often look for approval from others. In answering such questions, you will only provide them with a temporary ego boost, and your comments may only serve to further fuel their obsession with eating and weight. Tell your child that such questions make you worry about her, and that it's more important to you how she feels, not how she looks. Emphasize your child's qualities that you love, so that you can help boost her self-esteem by encouraging interactions that are supportive and affectionate.

Question: "I just feel so ashamed—it's probably my fault, so the last thing I should do is interfere now and make things worse."

Answer: Remember that you are still a parent. There are many, many factors that contribute to a person developing an eating disorder, so to say that it is "your fault" that your son or daughter became sick is probably not realistic. Additionally, it is not very helpful! Regardless of the different reasons your child is ill, you can still play a vital role in helping him or her get well. Blaming yourself is both useless and unfair. It will only make you feel rotten and less able to help your child, who needs you right now. The focus should be on moving forward, not just feeling regretful about the past. Consider talking to your child about your concerns and your desire that he or she seek help. If your child is an adolescent you may feel that you are not a helpful part of his or her life right now. Try to get past this feeling. Parents play a major role in shaping their children's lives and personalities.

Sally's Story

Sally, a nineteen-year-old student, was home from college for the summer when her family noticed that she was losing a lot of weight. Throughout high school, Sally had been concerned about her appearance and often tried the latest popular diets, but her weight had never dropped this low before. Her parents and sisters were concerned as they watched her skip meals and exercise for hours at a time even though she seemed very tired. Sally, however, insisted that her eating and exercise were healthy and fine. She did not understand her family's concerns, and this difference of opinion became a major source of conflict in the house.

Sally and her mother, Betty, started to have loud arguments during which Sally would cry and say things like "I'm fat and ugly. I need to lose weight, so leave me alone." Her mother would try to convince her otherwise, shouting back, "You're beautiful. You've always been thin and pretty and popular. I don't know what's wrong with you, but you're acting crazy." After repeatedly arguing like this, Sally's mother found herself frustrated and worried, so she contacted a psychologist specializing in eating disorders. Even though Sally refused to see a therapist and her father and sisters did not want to participate in therapy, her mother made an appointment to talk with a psychologist on her own.

Exhausted and feeling alone in her struggle to help her daughter, Betty told the therapist about the weight loss, excessive exercise, skipped meals, and arguments. She talked about not understanding why her daughter was acting the way she was, especially since her daughter was "strikingly beautiful" and "as thin as anyone would want to be." The therapist and Sally's mom agreed to meet weekly as a source of support and to help develop solutions for these difficulties.

With the therapist's help, Betty recognized that participating in arguments with Sally was resulting in louder and more frequent fights, without effectively conveying the things she really wanted her daughter to hear. The therapist's first recommendation involved finding ways to reduce the tension in the house by trying to eliminate arguments about shape, weight, and appearance. Sally's mother was encouraged to refrain from arguing with her daughter about how she looked and instead to try to identify and express her own feelings. During their meetings, the therapist and Sally's mother developed ways for her to communicate more effectively by using I statements like: "I'm worried about you and wish I could help you feel better," instead of trying to console Sally by insisting that she is thin. Betty learned that while she could not make her daughter feel better about her body by voicing an opposing opinion, she could change the way she interacted with Sally.

Betty and the therapist met for six weeks, which resulted in a less argumentative atmosphere in the home and the beginning of a calmer relationship between mother and daughter. With fewer and less intense arguments in the house, the family was able to talk more openly about their concerns, and eventually Sally agreed to have a physical exam to assess her health. Although she was still not convinced that she had a problem, Sally was more agreeable to her mother's suggestions when they were presented in a concerned, rather than argumentative, way. Betty felt an enormous sense of relief when her daughter agreed to make an appointment with a physician who specializes in eating disorders. Even though she knew that the road to recovery would be long and difficult for Sally, Betty was relieved to know that a medical professional would be assessing her daughter and offering recommendations for treatment.

Lucy's Story

Lucy was a sixteen-year-old high school student and the youngest in her family. Her older brother and sister no longer lived at home, but they visited frequently because the family enjoyed spending time together. Her brother, an investment banker, and her sister, a medical student, were described by Lucy as "perfect." They had both been straight-A students in high school, were never in trouble as teenagers, and always seemed to be great at whatever they tried. Even though

Lucy was also a high achiever with excellent grades, academic honors, and awards in showing horses, she had difficulty recognizing her own achievements and often felt like "a wallflower." Lucy tended to be quiet, and she rarely complained or argued.

When she started to see a therapist for her eating disorder, Lucy had a hard time talking about herself. She said that she didn't understand why she had an eating disorder because everything in her life was fine. She and her therapist focused first on monitoring her eating and decreasing her secret junk food binges, excessive exercise, and laxative use. As she became more comfortable in therapy and more able to eat without bingeing and purging, Lucy and her therapist started to focus on her feelings about herself as well as her relationships within her family. The psychologist recommended family therapy, but Lucy explained that she wouldn't feel comfortable talking about these concerns in front of her parents, who rarely acknowledged or discussed problems. Much like her description of her brother and sister, Lucy said that her parents never argued with each other, never raised their voices, and acted as though nothing was ever wrong. They often said to each other that they "never had any problems with the first two" and that they don't know why Lucy wouldn't eat normally.

Lucy's psychologist was concerned that the family's pattern of not recognizing problems could be a factor maintaining Lucy's disorder and influencing her poor self-image. Realizing that Lucy was not yet ready for family therapy, her therapist recommended that her parents attend an information session about eating disorders at the local hospital and consider joining a support group for parents so that they could better understand how to help their daughter. Lucy's parents reluctantly agreed to attend and were surprised to find that the lecture and the support session were very helpful. During the lecture, they learned about the symptoms of bulimia and anorexia as well as characteristics, such as perfectionism and self-criticism, associated with these problems. They listened to other parents talk about how they may have unwittingly communicated to their children a high expectation of achievement as well as disapproval of openly expressing negative feelings, such as anger. The parents involved in the group were concerned about their children and helped each other to generate ideas about how to improve communication patterns in their families.

After attending the group for a number of weeks, Lucy's parents started to talk about their tendency to avoid discussing upsetting topics and not sharing their problems for fear of burdening their children. As they became more comfortable talking with others in the group, they began to feel a sense of relief in not having to keep silent about their own worries. They started to understand that they may have inadvertently given Lucy the impression that it's not okay to talk about difficult feelings, such as disappointment, sadness, and anger. Together, Lucy's parents agreed that they would try to create a more open atmosphere in their home, where they would set an example of talking more openly about their own experiences and concerns. They hoped that Lucy and their two older children would participate in their efforts to be more open and direct with each other.

At first, Lucy and her siblings wondered why their parents were acting so strangely. It seemed like all of a sudden they wanted to talk about problems and initiate conversations about their feelings. This was unusual, and their three children found it a little unnerving. Eventually, however, Lucy, her brother, and sister recognized the value in their parents' efforts. Mostly, they felt that their parents really cared about them and were taking Lucy's eating disorder very seriously. Lucy was particularly touched that they would "go to all this trouble for me" and started to consider her psychologist's recommendation of family therapy. For Lucy, the most important change was that her parents seemed okay with asking others for help and with acknowledging that having difficulties is normal and acceptable.

Creating Solutions

We hope that the information provided in this chapter has helped you and your family to identify some new ways of communicating with each other. If you have come to realize that family members make many self-critical comments like "I feel so fat today," you may decide to work to avoid "fat talk" in the house. Instead, you can make a habit of commenting on ways you appreciate your body (for example, "Boy, my legs sure worked hard to get me to the bus stop on time this morning!") and noting other positive qualities about one another that do not focus on appearance. It may sound hokey, but the things we say to ourselves and our children have a tremendous impact on how we feel—consider the difference between saying "Ugh, my thighs are so fat!" versus "Wow, my legs just got me up those stairs for the tenth time today!"

Try writing down three ideas to try in your house for the next two weeks to improve family communication:

1._____

2._____

3._____

At the end of the two weeks, evaluate how the experiment turned out.

What were different family members' reactions?

_____

_____

_____

_____

_____

Think about whether you want to continue these new changes in your home. As you experiment with new strategies at home, keep in mind that this is a trial and error process to figure out the right approaches for your family. No one expects you to be perfect. We just hope you'll keep working together and trying new ways of communicating.

CHAPTER 5

What Can You Do at Home?
Dealing with Food, Diet, and Exercise

When Emily was a little girl, we used to love to walk to the ice cream parlor together on summer nights and have ice cream cones. Now, when I ask her if she wants to go get ice cream with me, she acts like I am asking her to break the law! All I really want is to spend some time with her. What am I supposed to do?

—Fred, father of a thirteen-year-old girl with anorexia nervosa

Food is central to images of family togetherness and celebration in our culture. Despite hectic schedules and the convenience of microwave dinners, many families still use mealtimes as a chance to reconnect after a day at work and school. Even our major holidays, such as Thanksgiving, Christmas, and Passover, feature food prominently with the expectation that the family will join together to celebrate and feast. One of the particularly devastating aspects of having a child with an eating disorder is that everything from family vacations to trips to the grocery store can become filled with conflict rather than enjoyment. Food is no longer a source of nourishment or pleasure; instead it causes frustration, anger, sadness, and fear.

In this chapter, we address common myths about food, diet, and exercise and talk about the requirements for a healthy meal plan. We also provide some practical advice on how to handle food issues in the home, such as shopping, storage, cooking, and mealtimes. In addition, we include strategies to help make sense of our society's obsession with dieting and exercise. We respond to frequently asked questions about food, diet, and exercise and include case examples to demonstrate different approaches to handling these complicated issues. Finally, we raise the challenge of understanding the connection your family makes between mood and food (that is, how feelings relate to eating habits), and help you monitor your own eating with a daily food record.

Debunking Myths about Food and Exercise

Myth: A child with eating problems will binge, no matter what foods are in the house.

Research says: There are certain foods that are more likely to be binge foods and cause trouble for your child. While it is true that a person can binge on any type of food, researchers have found that "binge foods" are often high in carbohydrates and low in protein. They include sweets (such as ice cream, cakes, and chocolates) and high fat foods (such as bread, butter, pasta, and cheese) (Van der Ster Wallin, Norring, and Holmgren 1994).

Myth: There is no such thing as too much exercise.

Research says: You can have too much of a good thing. While everyone needs to engage in some form of physical activity, excessive sport or exercise that is used to achieve an ideal body weight or shape, rather than to maintain physical and mental health, may be a symptom of an eating disorder. Some people with eating disorders use excessive exercise as an attempt to "cancel out" caloric intake (placing exercise in the same category as vomiting, laxative abuse, diuretic abuse, or fasting). (Beumont 2002). Excessive exercise can also lead to a range of physical problems and can slow down recovery from an eating disorder.

Myth: My daughter should just use her willpower and stick to a diet. This will enable her to stop binge eating and having to purge.

Research says: Fad diets and food rules are incompatible with recovery from eating disorders. We are bombarded every day by advertisements for miracle weight loss diets. Some diets tell you to eat low carbohydrate and high protein; others tell you to eat low fat and high carbohydrate. Still others dictate a low-sugar plan. There are plans devised to supposedly fit with your body type, your personality type, or even your blood type!

For every day of the year, there is a new and contradictory fad diet. Not only is there no evidence to support the effectiveness of these diets, but there is reason to believe that they are harmful, both physically and psychologically.

Starvation and fad diets are highly ineffective in maintaining long-term weight loss and are thought to be linked to the onset of bingeing and purging. Further, diets that are too low in fat may not be as effective in weight loss as once believed.

Do not be fooled by misleading advertising. U.S industries have a great incentive to promote the weight loss message. Americans spend billions of dollars every year on diet-related products and programs (Brownell 1991).

What Is Healthy Eating?

Eating disorders often begin as a restrictive diet, and an important part of recovery is learning healthy eating behaviors. You can help your child by knowing how to eat in a healthy way and by making nutritious food choices available for your entire family.

Our bodies need food for fuel; starvation or the elimination of any entire food group is not healthy and has serious medical consequences. We all need to eat a balance of fat, protein, and carbohydrates each day, and the best-supported nutritional plan is the food guide pyramid put out by the U.S. Department of Agriculture (USDA). This guide suggests that a person consume meals that combine all five food groups: grains, fruits, vegetables, meat, and milk. The goal is for you to enjoy a range of foods that you like, while also taking care of your body.

The three key factors to keep in mind for a healthy diet are variety, balance, and moderation. One should aim to have a daily fat intake that averages approximately 30 percent of the total calories consumed per day. Although the food guide pyramid recommends consuming fats, oils, and sweets sparingly, remember that some fat is necessary for the maintenance of health. Fat provides us with an important source of energy, it aids in our growth, it maintains the structure of all of our cells, and it facilitates the absorption of vitamins A, D, E, and K (International Food and Information Council Foundation 1998).

For the other food groups, the U.S. Department of Agriculture (USDA 1996) and the Department of Health and Human Services receommend the following number of servings for each day:

Food Group	Number of Servings	Sample servings
Breads, cereals, rice, and pasta	6–11	1 slice bread, 1/2 bagel, 2–4 crackers, 1/2 cup cooked rice or pasta
Fruits	2–4	1 medium fruit (apple, banana, orange), 1/2 cup fruit juice, 1/2 cup cooked/canned fruit
Vegetables	3–5	1 cup raw leafy vegetables (lettuce, spinach), 1/2 cup cooked vegetables
Meat, poultry, fish, dry beans, eggs, and nuts	2–3	2–3 ounces cooked lean meat, fish, or skinless poultry; 1 egg
Milk, yogurt, and cheese	2–3	1 cup milk or yogurt, 2 ounces processed cheese

At the end of this chapter, we will give you an exercise to help you see how your eating compares to these recommendations.

How to Handle Food: Shopping, Storage, Cooking, and Mealtimes

The families we see often ask for guidance on managing food at home. During the recovery period, families frequently feel confused about how to handle day-to-day practical issues, such as grocery shopping, where to keep food, and what to do about cooking responsibilities and mealtimes. While there is no one right way to handle these issues, we can provide you with some guidelines. As with all the recommendations in this book, we suggest that you try these approaches for a couple of weeks and then check in with your family to see how effectively they are working.

Shopping Tips

In general, we suggest that you continue to buy the foods your family enjoys and typically eats, because this will cause the least disruption to your household and minimize frustration among other family members. The only foods you should probably avoid are the foods that your child eats during binge episodes. Having tempting foods around the house makes it harder for people with bulimia to avoid binge eating. In fact, even just seeing or smelling binge foods can create urges to binge that are hard to resist. Thus, we often recommend that families view recovery as a series of progressive stages. Initially it may be helpful to remove all binge foods from the house to reduce temptation. You will slowly be able to reintroduce these foods as treatment continues.

We recommend asking your child and you may also want to consider consulting with a therapist or dietician to help you decide how this issue can best be handled based on your child's stage of recovery. You might begin a discussion with these questions. Take notes.

- Which foods are most tempting for your child? _____

_____

- What would your child like your family to do about having (or not having) these foods in the house? _____

_____

_____

Once you have a sense of which food-shopping strategies would best support your child's effort not to binge, you can determine how this will impact other family members. For example, other children in the house may love sweet cereals and would feel resentful if these were no longer available at home because of their sibling. Try to reach a compromise that everyone in the household can accept. One approach may be to buy only small amounts of typical binge foods that other family members can keep in their own rooms so that the child who binges will not be tempted. In general, binge foods (i.e., junk food) are usually not healthy choices for anyone. To promote healthy eating in the whole family, it makes sense to limit these foods in the house.

You can also ask the family these questions:

- What foods would other family members like to have in the house? _____

_____

- What are some ways to compromise that are acceptable to everyone? _____

_____

- Which junk foods can you eliminate from your shopping list?

_____

Who Should Do the Grocery Shopping?

People with eating disorders vary in their responses to food shopping. For some, food shopping is a nightmare and very upsetting because eating disorder symptoms are triggered at the store. For others, this task is not emotionally difficult, but they may be tempted to buy only limited "diet" foods for the whole family.

The key to deciding who should shop is communication. Try to determine what role food shopping plays in your child's symptoms. If going to the grocery store is normally a part of your child's household responsibilities, ask if your child wishes to continue this task or be given a different task. (Note: your child is still responsible for contributing to the chore list with this approach.) It is important that all family members know what is expected of them in very clear and concrete terms.

Try to approach solutions to these problems as experiments. For example, you can try having your child continue the shopping, but at the next family meeting check in with everyone to see how effectively it is working. Your child may tell you that it is difficult to go to the grocery store, so that job may be given to someone else. The goal is to find a system that is nonpunitive and best facilitates the family's functioning. Not surprisingly, this involves a lot of trial and error, so regular family discussions are important.

Storage Issues

For some families, it seems impossible to keep potential binge foods out of the house. Sometimes other children will buy their own junk food with their allowance. Changes in shopping can also increase conflict among family members so that parents break down and reintroduce junk food into the house. In this case, if food is in the house, where should it be kept?

Storing Tempting Foods

Our policy is to always encourage honest communication. Therefore, if your child asks you directly about whether or not a particular food is in the house, we suggest you respond honestly. Otherwise, it is easy to set up a cycle of lying and mistrust in the family. With that said, some people with eating disorders prefer not to know that tempting binge foods are nearby. Thus, one solution is to keep these foods out of the kitchen or obvious communal areas, allowing other family members to keep these foods in their bedrooms or in a private place.

Keep in mind that early on in treatment even eating small amounts of typical binge foods can make someone with bulimia feel out of control and believe they have "broken the rules," which can in turn set them up to binge and purge. However, treatment is designed to help the individual learn that she or he can have normal portions of former "binge" foods, so over time these issues should become less of a problem in the family.

Think about these questions in advance of shopping, so you can prevent misunderstandings from occurring.

- Where can tempting foods be stored? _____

_____

- What does your child want to know about the storage of these foods? _____

_____

Monitoring Others' Eating

Parents often feel unsure about what role they should play in policing the kitchen. Some opt for a completely hands-off approach; everyone eats what they want, when they want, and parents do not plan family meals or check on nutrition. Other parents go to extreme lengths and actually place a lock on the kitchen cabinets and fridge so they can control access to food in the house. We recommend a compromise between these extremes. Planning meals and eating together once a day as a family will allow you to do some monitoring and will model healthy eating for your child in a positive environment. At the same time, this approach does not place you in an uncomfortable role where your children constantly need to ask permission to eat. Keep in mind that food should be a natural part of life, not a reward that is only given for good behavior.

Locking up food or excessively tracking each item seems like an extreme measure and does not fit with our philosophy of open communication and trust. One problem with trying to prevent your child from eating is that your child may simply go out of the house to get food. Outside of the home, the most readily available foods (those at convenience stores or in vending machines) are not nutritious.

- What is your family's style regarding planning meals and eating together? _____

_____

- What are the advantages and disadvantages of this style?

Advantages   **Disadvantages**

_____   _____

_____   _____

_____   _____

_____   _____

In rare cases, a child may directly ask for food sources to be locked up to help avoid binge eating. In this case, you may choose to grant your child's request. Try the locked doors for a one-week trial period, and then check in with one another to see how comfortable you feel with the system and to determine if the strategy really is helping to reduce binge eating. Here are some questions to help you think through these challenging issues:

- Has your child made any requests about monitoring his or her eating, locking cabinets, or changing the way your family usually handles these issues? _____

- If so, which of these requests seem reasonable to you? _____

_____

_____

- After trying a new approach that your child wants and that seems reasonable, try to evaluate whether or not it is useful. What did your child like and dislike about it? What did you like and dislike about it? _____

_____

_____

Cooking Questions

Parents are sometimes worried that asking their child to cook may exacerbate eating disorder symptoms because it involves working around food. Another concern is that the child will cook meals that do not appeal to other family members. Yet another is that people with eating disorders sometimes create elaborate meals for others but then do not eat the food themselves. Some parents become frustrated about the mess their child makes when preparing binge foods.

Should Someone with an Eating Disorder Cook?

Many parents assume that if their child has bulimia, involvement with food preparation will lead to bingeing. Rather than assume that this is the case for your child, ask what sort of arrangement would make your child feel most comfortable. It may be, for example, that cooking the main course tempts your child to binge but preparing the salad is not a problem. If this is true, then you can still share the cooking jobs so that the entire burden is not on your shoulders. By allowing your child to participate in the decision-making process and having calm discussions about food, you can demonstrate that food is a healthy, positive part of life.

Think about the following issues:

- Who usually cooks in your family? _____

- What does your child say about wanting to cook? _____

_____

Cooking for the Whole Family

One common complaint from parents is that their child with an eating disorder only wants to prepare fat-free meals for the family, while the rest of the family does not like fat-free food. Parents feel confused about how much they should dictate the type of meal their child prepares. We typically recommend that parents handle this issue for their child as a matter of general family policy. For example, when it is their turn to cook, are other members of the household expected to cook meals that appeal to everyone? If not, then it seems unfair to enforce this stricture only for the child with the eating disorder. However, if the "chef" for the evening is generally expected to prepare a meal that will appeal to most of the family, then it is reasonable to encourage your child to expand his or her repertoire to accommodate everyone.

One option is that your child could make one meal for the family and a different one for him- or herself (a workable but not ideal solution). Alternatively, your child could try to compromise and prepare a meal that consists of the foods that the family generally enjoys along with some fat-free foods that your child specifically wants. Family members could then choose whatever appeals to them. The good news is that there are many cookbooks available now that contain great-tasting, healthy recipes, so it may be possible for everyone's needs to be met.

What are some options that might work for your family?

_____

_____

_____

Cleaning Up after Cooking

All families have to negotiate responsibility for cleaning up after cooking, but it becomes more complicated when your child makes a mess while preparing food for a binge. In this case, parents often feel frustrated about the mess but unsure about insisting that their child clean up if he or she is already upset because of the binge episode. We recommend that you try to send a consistent message of love and support, but also reinforce that everyone in the family has to take responsibility for cleaning up their own messes in the kitchen.

We realize how painful it is to watch your child binge and know how upset your child is about this behavior; however, your child still needs to take appropriate responsibility. There are important strategies you can keep in mind. Try to respond in a way that will not seem like a punishment to your child for being ill. Make sure that you try to meet the emotional needs of your child before addressing the issue of the messy kitchen. For example, you may choose not to talk to your child about cleaning up the kitchen until hours after the binge episode has occurred because you need to address other concerns.

You will also want to be sensitive to the impact of the dirty kitchen on the rest of the household. For instance, if you are having a dinner party soon after the binge and you need the kitchen to be clean, you might suggest to your child that you swap chores. You could tell your child that you recognize how upset everyone feels right now, so you will clean the kitchen today with the expectation that he or she will take your turn washing the dishes tomorrow. The goal here is to help your child develop independence and responsibility without being punitive or shaming.

Consider the following questions about household responsiblities:

- What are each person's responsibilities for cleaning up the kitchen? _____

_____

_____

_____

- In what ways has cleaning the kitchen been problematic in your family? _____

_____

_____

_____

- What can you do to address these problems? _____

_____

_____

_____

Mealtime Concerns

Mealtimes are important and you want to make them a positive experience. Ideally, you want to make this time feel safe and non-confrontational and encourage your child with the eating disorder to join the rest of the family during mealtimes. The more regularly you can sit down together to enjoy a meal, the more you can create an atmosphere that promotes healthy eating for your child. Here are some ideas to address the common barriers to enjoying peaceful family meals together.

Sitting Down Together

Due to work schedules and school activities, many families have a hard time having dinner together every night. We realize that there are many competing demands for everyone's time, but there is no substitute for spending some time each day together as a family. Do your best to schedule family dinners and make them a priority.

Parents often tell us they are tempted to stop family meals altogether when their child is ill because of the stress around food during this time. These feelings of frustration and confusion are understandable, but a program of regular eating is important for recovery. Try to have dinners together as much as possible so that your child can see a normal pattern of positive, social eating. Even if your child refuses to eat, extend an invitation to sit at the table with the rest of the family. Recovery happens in gradual stages. Therefore, promote any behaviors that move in the direction of regular eating. For example, if during the initial stage of therapy, your child does not want to eat what the rest of the family is having, allow your child to prepare other food but invite him or her to sit down with the rest of the family to eat it.

Here are some questions to help you start planning family meals:

- What nights this week can your family sit down together for dinner? _____

_____

- On what days can your family have breakfast or lunch together this week? _____

_____

Keeping the Peace

Many families find that mealtimes explode into arguments because they are the only time the family sits down and tells each other things they are upset about. The stress of being around food and watching one another eat when one person at the table has an eating disorder can also exacerbate hurt feelings. Rather than abandoning family dinners, try to avoid discussing business and family problems at the dinner table and keep the conversation at dinner on neutral issues that promote a positive environment. This strategy can often reduce mealtime stress and conflict.

It may be useful to plan separate family meetings to openly discuss problems. Consider family discussions in your home:

- What are the topics that your family usually discusses during mealtimes? _____

_____

_____

- What are some additional topics you could discuss at family meals to make your time together as enjoyable as possible?

_____

_____

Dining Out

Parents often feel especially sensitive to fights that occur over going out to dinner because they feel that taking the family out to eat should be a treat. Try to keep in mind that the negative reaction from your child with the eating disorder is due to the disorder, not a rejection of your attempt to do something nice with your family.

When considering dining out, you want to encourage normal functioning as much as possible. The rest of the family should not be denied the pleasure of dining out or entertaining, but try to respect your child's wishes regarding participation. Keep in mind that your child's tolerance and openness to these experiences will likely change over time. Do not be disheartened by initial refusals, and continue to invite your child to join in.

Ask yourself the following questions:

- How does your child react to eating in restaurants? _____

_____

- What can you do to decrease the arguments or tension about this problem? _____

_____

Making Sense of the Dieting and Exercise Craze

Parents often come to us feeling confused about the mixed messages they get from the media. On the one hand, every other magazine ad talks about a new diet or exercise program that will make you look and feel better. Meanwhile, almost everyone has friends, colleagues, or other family members who are willing to swear by the powers of some new diet they have tried or a great new workout regime. On the other hand, eating disorder therapists point out the serious dangers of following extreme diets and the use of excessive exercise to compensate for perceived overeating.

Who's correct? The magic word to keep in mind is moderation. Exercise is one of the best things you can do to benefit your health, but people run into trouble when working out involves agonizing efforts to lose weight or change their body shape. Similarly, eating a balanced diet that includes a limited number of sweets is a great way to maintain good health, but severely restricting your food intake or cutting out certain food groups completely is dangerous.

Getting Exercise

There is a difference between the use of exercise for health and the compulsive need to exercise that is part of an eating disorder. Exercise is appropriate when it helps increase vitality and strength—not when it leads to weakness or malnutrition.

Here are some questions to determine if your child is over-exercising:

- Is your child exercising more than an hour a day of solitary, extremely strenuous exercise?

- Does exercise get in the way of participating in other activities, like being with friends or doing homework?

- Is the focus on the number of calories being burned?

- Does your child exercise even when injured, sick, or the weather is bad?

If you answered "yes" to any of these questions, exercise may have become a symptom of the eating disorder. If this is the case, consult with a professional to devise a safe exercise plan for each stage of your child's recovery. Sometimes an underweight person must stop exercising entirely in the beginning. Over time, moderate exercise is usually fine if your child is physically healthy and exercise is approved by his or her physician. If your child is currently at a normal weight and is not using excessive exercise as a method of compensating for binge eating, a moderate exercise program can probably continue. As always, we encourage you to bring any questions you might have about your child's health to a trained medical professional.

The Dangers of Dieting

Parents often find it difficult to set limits when their child wants to go on a diet, especially if they do not think their child is underweight. We suggest that you help your child learn about the benefits of healthy nutrition and the danger and ineffectiveness of rigid dieting. Let your child know that crash diets rarely lead to sustained weight loss and discuss the health risks of denying your body what it needs.

You can demonstrate healthy eating by encouraging all members of the family to follow the food guide pyramid (described earlier) and to eat three balanced meals a day with two or three snacks. No one likes to be lectured—especially young people—so demonstrating healthy living may be the best way to help your child learn healthy habits. At the very least, this will give your child an alternative to the rigid yo-yo dieting her or his friends are doing, plus you will be promoting your own health at the same time.

It can also be helpful to start educating your child about the dangers of fad diets. Some diet plans are more healthy than others. As a general guideline, we recommend that you look for scientific evidence showing that a diet plan is nourishing and beneficial in the long term. Almost any fad diet can make a claim about one person who lost a large amount of weight, but you want to see evidence of maintained fitness and a sustained healthy weight. Also, look at how the diet is being advertised. Was it developed by individuals with solid credentials in nutrition and medicine, or are celebrities showing off their thin bodies in magazines to make the diet look tempting? Finally, consider how closely the diet program matches the food guide pyramid developed by the USDA.

If you want to know more about a particular diet, do your research. The U.S. Department of Agriculture, the American Heart Association, and the American Dietetic Association often come out with useful information. For example, the American Dietetic Association has stated that "fad diets are a short-term, quick-fix approach to weight loss that don't work over the long haul." Fad diets can be dangerous for your health; for example, high protein, low carbohydrate diets "can result in dehydration, diarrhea, weakness, headaches, bad breath, and dizziness, and can also increase the risk of atherosclerosis and osteoporosis" (International Food Information Council Foundation 2000). Be a smart consumer.

Questions and Answers about Food, Diet, and Exercise

Question: "My son says that he only wants me to buy very particular items at the store since these are the only foods he feels comfortable eating. The problem is that he wants only expensive low-fat foods, which are dramatically increasing the cost of our grocery budget. We desperately want him to eat, so should we go along with his requests, despite the financial burden?"

Answer: While you want to do everything you can to help your son, you need to take care of yourself and other members of the family as well. It is not reasonable for his food demands to put a financial strain on the family. In addition, eating disorders involve a pervasive preoccupation with shape and weight, so no single food purchase can make an eating disorder go away. If there are medical reasons why your child needs to eat particular foods, then that is a separate issue. However, if picky eating is occurring because of the eating disorder, then you should not feel guilty about setting some limits. Sometimes a child will insist on a particular brand of food—not infrequently the most expensive one at the store. In this case, you may try to negotiate a compromise, buying that brand some weeks, but trying a few other brands to find others that are acceptable.

Another strategy would be to give your son a food budget that can be used to choose one or two special items each week. If it is feasible financially, you could also allow each family member to select one special item per week to add to the shopping cart, so that your son is not singled out for special treatment. If you decide that you simply cannot afford to increase the costs of your food bill, you should not believe that you are perpetuating the eating disorder. Your child is preoccupied with food, and these preoccupations are guiding his eating problems, not the particular items in the shopping cart.

Question: "My husband really likes having food around that he can grab and eat on the run, but this is often the same food that my daughter eats during binges. Would it be helpful to keep food in the house that requires some preparation, rather than having so many ready-to-eat foods?"

Answer: This strategy may be helpful to slow down or prevent binges that occur impulsively, or when your daughter is eating automatically without really being aware of her food intake. Having frozen foods, which at least require some cooking time, may help her break the binge cycle before she has begun to eat. Certainly, it is much easier to quickly sneak down to the kitchen and eat a carton of ice cream than it is to defrost a pizza and cook it. If your daughter plans her binges ahead of time, however, this strategy may not be as helpful in decreasing the number of binge episodes. Again, we recommend asking your daughter and her therapist about this plan. In addition, talk to your husband about whether or not he can live without his ready-to-eat foods. Perhaps you can identify a store nearby where he can still grab food on the run.

Question: "My daughter has become a master chef. She spends hours poring over cookbooks and preparing elaborate meals for our family. The problem is that she never eats the food herself, and I feel like she is spending all of her time in the kitchen. I don't want to hurt her feelings, but how can I tell her to stop?"

Answer: Sometimes individuals with eating disorders (especially anorexia nervosa) develop a preoccupation with cooking meals for others. This is connected to their general preoccupation with food. Explain to your daughter that you see this behavior as part of the disorder, and you would like her to take a break from making these types of meals for the family for a while. As she recovers, you can invite her to make foods that she will eat with the family. Eventually, depending on how her recovery progresses, she may be able to resume making meals as well as joining the family in enjoying them.

Question: "Every New Year's Day I resolve to start a new diet and join the gym, but I'm not sure how this affects my daughter who is overly thin and preoccupied with her weight. How much emphasis should we place on exercising and eating healthily as a family?"

Answer: Eating a balanced diet and promoting moderate regular exercise are positive goals for all members of the family, including your child. However, it is important to focus on these activities as a way of maintaining health, rather than to emphasize their effect on appearance. Once you confirm that it is safe for your daughter to participate in physical activity, try to plan fun family events like skating, skiing, hiking, or biking so that you can enjoy the activity and de-emphasize the use of exercise to lose weight.

Question: "All of the magazines show pictures of men with very little body fat, so why is it wrong for my son to want to lose weight if he is overweight?"

Answer: In general, it is recommended that people who are overweight and suffer from bulimia should first regulate their eating and stop binge eating and purging (O'Connor, Touyz, and Beumont 1988). Once the person has successfully followed a pattern of regular eating, he or she may make dietary changes to facilitate gradual weight loss. It is helpful to work with a nutritionist to make these changes. The first goal in treatment is to focus on being healthy and recovering from the eating disorder. Once this has been accomplished, it is reasonable to aim for weight loss if your child is significantly overweight, given that being overweight is a health risk in its own right. In fact, the methods encouraging healthy weight loss are similar to those promoting recovery from an eating disorder: eat a balanced diet and engage in moderate regular exercise. Again, try not to focus on your son's physical appearance. Your child can eat a healthy diet and be physically active, but he still may never look like the men in the magazines. You can help by letting him know how proud you are of the healthy changes he is making and by de-emphasizing the importance of looking like a model.

Pam's Story

As a seventeen-year-old senior in high school, Pam sought treatment for her eating disorder at the insistence of her parents. Her bingeing and vomiting had gotten out of control over the course of five months. One particularly difficult aspect of her eating disorder in terms of family dynamics was that Pam would binge on snack foods that belonged to the entire family. Her two younger brothers and one younger sister were upset that their after-school snacks were disappearing, and Pam's parents were worried about the extent to which the family was arguing and disagreeing about how to handle this problem.

Pam's therapist suggested that the family choose a weekday evening to sit down together after dinner to discuss the matter. Pam requested that binge foods be kept out of the house, but her siblings adamantly refused. They insisted that not having snacks in the house was unfair to them. As a compromise, the family decided that snacks would be allowed in the house but that they would be kept out of common areas and hidden from Pam in other people's bedrooms.

For some families, this strategy works, but in Pam's family arguing about food continued, only in a different form. Though snacks were not available in the kitchen, Pam knew that they were hidden in the house, which resulted in her searching the rooms of her brothers and sister when she wanted to binge. This, in turn, led to arguments about privacy and trust. Although this strategy didn't work, it's important to note that Pam's family had made some headway. They had discussed a problem, identified a possible solution, and tried it out. The next step for Pam and her family would be to have another meeting in order to re-negotiate how to store food. One idea would be for the family to keep snacks out of the house for a short, predetermined period. Although Pam's brothers and sister might be opposed to keeping snacks out of the house for a long time, they might agree to try it for two or three weeks. In addition, they could be given an allowance for buying treats away from home. During this trial period, the family could assess the usefulness of this strategy for everyone. Pam might be able to reduce her binge eating and purging, while her brothers and sister might benefit from having fewer arguments and disappointments regarding food.

Matt's Story

Matt was a sixteen-year-old student who had been hiding his bulimia from his friends and family for three years. Although he regularly purged following binge episodes, and even occasionally vomited after eating small amounts of food, he frequently felt very guilty if he did not also exercise following a large meal. His desire to exercise was entirely fueled by fears of weight gain, and he had little concern about overall health, instead wishing to "burn calories and fat to make up for eating like a pig."

Matt spent a large sum of money on a treadmill for his room. He even used up the money he had hoped to put toward a car, because he felt that right now nothing was more important than exercising. After eating each night, he would spend over an hour running on the treadmill, anxiously watching the "calories burned" total on the monitor. He told himself that he needed to burn off as many calories as he had eaten that day, but he always had to stop due to exhaustion before he reached his goal.

When Matt entered therapy, he spoke with his therapist about his guilt regarding exercise and the attempts he had previously made to follow a rigid exercise schedule. They discussed the value of physical activity to promote health rather than to compensate for eating. They talked about realistic fitness guidelines to address Matt's misperceptions about what constituted reasonable (rather than excessive) exercise. In addition, the therapist worked with Matt to determine how exercise could fit into and enhance his lifestyle, instead of being a guilt-driven activity.

In talking with his therapist, Matt decided that it was important for him not to spend lots of money on exercise, and he began to want exercise to feel fun and social, rather than painful and isolated, as it had in the past. Matt decided to contact friends to set up shared activities. He arranged a roller-blading date for Saturday afternoons with the person he was dating, and he planned to play soccer after school with friends one day a week. Recognizing that he found it difficult to stick with any particular exercise for long, Matt decided he would try this new plan for a month, then reevaluate it.

Creating Solutions

In this chapter, we have discussed food shopping, storage, cooking, and mealtimes, as well as challenges related to diet and exercise. Each family has its own style of handling food and unique ways of connecting food with emotion or rewards. Some of these ways can be healthy, such as a grandparent who likes to bake cookies for their grandchildren as a sign of love. Other ways can be less healthy, such as using food as a reward for a desired behavior or withholding it as a punishment. For example, some parents let their children have dessert only if they do well on a test in school, and others do not allow their children to buy candy at the movies if they make too much noise in the car.

Now would be a good time to think about what food and exercise mean to you and your family. Part of the connection between mood and food concerns who plays what roles in determining eating patterns in your family. The other part of the connection concerns how eating is used to respond to different moods (such as eating more or less when you are upset). Here are some questions regarding family roles and food to help you think about these issues:

- Who does the shopping and preparing of foods?
- Who cleans up?
- How is the shopping list made?
- How are menu selections made?
- What is the favorite meal of each family member?
- How often do you eat dinner as a family?
- How often do family members try new fad diets?
- What is the atmosphere of family meals?
- How have your mealtimes been impacted by your child's eating disorder?

Similarly, issues related to fitness and exercise can become very tense or emotional when a family member has an eating disorder.

- How has your comfort with exercise been impacted by your child's eating disorder?
- How often do people in your family exercise?
- Do family members exercise for health or for appearance?
- Are there ways to incorporate exercise into your lifestyle so that it can be an enjoyable part of each day (such as walking the dog, taking the stairs)?

In thinking about what food and mealtimes mean to you, it is sometimes useful to think back to your own childhood to identify what you liked (and did not like) about the way things were handled by your parents.

- What memories do you have about the foods that were available in your home?
- Was food ever used as a reward or punishment?
- Was food intake monitored, or could family members eat however much or little they wanted?
- Was the dinner table quiet or rambunctious?
- What do you remember about your family meals while growing up?

- Are there certain holiday dishes you remember?

Connecting Mood and Food

As your child is recovering, try to work as a family to spend some time together eating meals. While this may be a challenge, clear communication and compromise can assist your family in finding guidelines that work for everyone. Part of this communication will include telling each other what mealtimes have felt like in the past and what you would like from them in the future. This can include practical issues (such as the time of the meal), interpersonal issues (including what the conversation is about), and specific food issues (for example, what is served, how it is served). Try to discuss each person's preferences for a family meal.

Creating solutions is a process that requires trial and error. One way to think about this is to do a series of experiments in your family. Take the above information about each family member's meal preferences and come up with three possible scenarios that you would like to try this week (such as eating Sunday brunch together). As a family, decide to give each scenario an honest effort and see what it feels like.

Come up with three possible mealtime ideas to try:

1. _____

2. _____

3. _____

After the experimental meals are over, have a family meeting to discuss how it went from each person's perspective. You can also use this trial and error approach to think about ideas for exercise to try in your family, such as planning a fun physical activity that you can do together to promote health (like going for a hike). Remember to keep the focus on moderate exercise for the benefit of health, rather than weight loss.

Come up with three possible exercise plans to try:

1. _____

2. _____

3. _____

Keep a Food Record

As you and your family make these positive changes in your eating and exercise habits, you can monitor part of your progress by keeping track of your eating. Food records are often an essential part of treatment because they help to increase awareness of food choices and the factors linked to extreme restriction or out-of-control eating episodes. It is not useful to take on the role of therapist in monitoring your child's eating. However, you may want to try keeping these records for yourself for a little while, so that you can learn how your eating matches the recommendations of the food guide pyramid. The idea is not to become preoccupied with what you are eating, but to increase awareness of how many servings you are having of each food group and see where you can make healthy changes in your eating habits.

We have provided a sample daily food record in appendix B. There are many different ways to track your eating and varying levels of specificity. Here are some tips:

- Try to be specific about the foods you eat. Listing "chicken and vegetables" for dinner does not provide a lot of information because the way the food is prepared and the amount eaten make a big difference to the healthfulness of the meal. For example, five Kentucky Fried Chicken wings and a pint of creamy coleslaw have very different nutritional values than a three ounce grilled chicken breast with no skin and a cup of steamed broccoli.

- Keep track of the locations where you eat. You can pay attention to patterns involving, for example, how often you eat at your desk or in the car, how frequently you eat together as a family, and how often you eat in restaurants. Under what circumstances do you make better or worse nutritional choices? Feel satisfied after the meal? By identifying patterns such as these, you can determine changes you'd like to make as well as healthy behaviors that are already in place. Knowing your nutritional strengths and weaknesses can be valuable in developing long-lasting, healthy eating habits.

- Do your best to keep track of your eating so that you can learn to make healthier choices and raise your awareness of your own and your family's eating habits. Make sure, however, that the monitoring is playing a positive (rather than obsessive or self-critical) role in your life.

CHAPTER 6

What Happens in Treatment?
*Different Types of Therapy
and Your Role*

*Bringing my child to a therapist required a huge leap of faith.
Here I was, trusting someone else to help my child, when I
hadn't been able to help him myself. I was caught between
wanting the therapist to fix him quickly, yet worrying that if he
did, it would show that I should have been able to do it myself
all along.*

—Kate, parent of an eighteen-year-old with
    anorexia nervosa

One of your most important roles is to make sure your child gets the
expert help he or she needs. You may feel that your child's psychological health is your responsibility and not the responsibility of outside
professionals. This misconception results in part from the stigma associated with mental illness—parts of our society still think that psychological problems are not "real" problems but are the fault of the individual
or the family. This is simply wrong. It is important to make sure your
child knows that you view the eating disorder as an illness that needs
professional treatment.

Finding help for your child may require research, trial and error,
and patience. Ultimately though, it should bring a great reward—a step
toward your child's recovery. The process can be complicated by

confusion about the rights and responsibilities of the child and the parents. For example, most of the time, parents pay for treatment, yet the child is the one who is attending the sessions. This sets up the potential for conflict, because parents are paying for a service that they are not able to observe or monitor directly. The aim of this chapter is to address a range of concerns and questions that parents have about therapy. At the end of the chapter, we include a guide for developing a treatment contract with your child's therapist so that you can set up clear expectations from the beginning about what your role will be in your child's treatment.

Debunking Myths about Treatment

Myth: The therapist will turn your child against you and take away all of your control as a parent.

Research says: Whether your child is in treatment or not, you still have influence as a parent. Therapists and parents play very different roles in a child's life. No therapy can or should take over your role as a parent. Keep in mind that you and your child's therapist want the same thing— recovery for your child. An effective therapist will work with you, not against you. Furthermore, the goal should be to make positive changes for the future, not to blame anyone for the past.

It is not uncommon for parents to worry that they will be blamed for their family member's illness. Therapy should not be about turning family members against one another. If it feels like this is happening, say something to the therapist and discuss strategies for addressing this together. Try to be open to making changes in your family life if your child's therapist suggests it. Testing these new suggestions does not mean that you are giving up your role as a parent; it should help you become an even better parent. A survey of people seeing mental health professionals found that, overall, people report positive experiences. Specifically people reported feeling respected and listened to by their therapists, as well as feeling that the therapist explained things clearly to them (Eisen, et al. 1991). Remember, if you are not happy with the treatment your family is receiving, you do have the option of selecting a new therapist. You should never feel trapped.

Myth: Once your child starts treatment, everybody will think he's crazy and no one will look at him the same way.

Research says: If you let your own embarrassment hold your child back from treatment, his chances for recovery are greatly reduced. It is understandable that families with mentally ill members experience a wide range of emotions, including fear, shame, guilt, compassion, and secrecy over mental health care. However, you can play a valuable role in helping to take away the stigma of mental illness for your child by helping him or her seek professional care.

Try to be an advocate for your child and fight against the stereotypes about mental illness that exist in our society. You may want to take advantage of support and advocacy groups in your local area to help you through this difficult time.

What to Expect in Treatment

The good news is that there are many different treatment options available; the bad news is that it isn't always clear which approach is best for your child. Treatment for eating disorders can take the form of individual therapy, group therapy, or family therapy. Treatment often requires a team of experts working together, which can include a psychologist or social worker, a nutritionist, a psychiatrist, and a family doctor. Community support groups may be helpful as well.

Different Types of Therapy

Regardless of the format chosen for your child (individual, group, or family therapy), the type of psychological treatment he or she receives will likely be one of the models listed below. The approaches with the most research support indicating their effectiveness in treating eating disorders are cognitive behavioral therapy (CBT) and interpersonal therapy (IPT). Many therapists consider themselves "eclectic," which means that they utilize strategies from a variety of treatment approaches. It is reasonable for you to ask therapists to explain their treatment approach, the theory behind it, and how they assess progress. In this section, we have briefly summarized the philosophies behind the major treatment approaches and noted some of the key research findings supporting their effectiveness.

Following each description, we have provided some space for you to take notes on your perception of this particular therapy's advantages and disadvantages. Use this space to help think through the therapy options that feel right for your child and your family and to note any further questions you have.

Cognitive Behavioral Therapy

Cognitive behavioral treatment (CBT) for bulimia is based on the idea that as a consequence of low self-esteem and societal pressures to be thin, an individual comes to place undue importance on body shape and weight. This leads to strict and rigid dieting, which makes an individual both psychologically and physiologically vulnerable to periodic loss of control over eating (binge eating). Following a binge, the person is likely to feel guilty for the loss of control and use purging (such as vomiting or other compensatory behaviors) to counteract the effects of the binge episode. These behaviors in turn intensify low self-esteem and preoccupation with shape and weight, reinforcing a painful cycle. The goal in treatment is to replace the rigid dieting with normal, healthy eating patterns and to change the hurtful thoughts and feelings about the importance of shape and weight (Wilson, Fairburn, and Agras 1997).

Research support: Because of the strong research evidence demonstrating the effectiveness of CBT for eating disorders, this is the form of therapy used most frequently at the Yale Center for Eating and Weight Disorders. CBT has been found to reduce binge eating and purging by an average of about 75 percent (Peterson and Mitchell 1999). Although promising new treatment approaches are constantly in development, CBT for the treatment of anorexia nervosa has not shown the same level of success as it has for bulimia nervosa. There is some evidence, however, that in comparison to other forms of treatment, such as nutritional therapy or drug therapy used alone, CBT may be more effective in the later stages of recovery for anorexia once a person's weight has been restored to a healthier level (Vitousek 2002). There is also evidence suggesting that CBT can effectively treat binge eating disorder (Wilfley 2002).

Your Ideas

Advantages:_____

_____

_____

Disadvantages: _____

_____

_____

Questions: _____

_____

_____

Interpersonal Therapy (IPT)

In interpersonal therapy (IPT), the emphasis is on helping the individual to identify and modify current interpersonal problems. The goal of this type of treatment is to change the aspects of interpersonal functioning that maintain the disorder. The focus is not on eating behaviors specifically, but on a particular problem area in the person's relationships (Fairburn 1997). As we pointed out in chapter 3, in IPT, one of four interpersonal problem areas is typically identified as the primary problem in the person's life. The four areas are grief, interpersonal disputes (such as conflict with another person), transitions (such as starting college or leaving home), or interpersonal deficits (including not having enough social support). By examining the interpersonal problem, the client gains perspective, and this understanding is then used to change the unhealthy pattern of relating.

Research support: There is scientific support for the use of IPT to treat bulimia nervosa (Fairburn 1997). As a treatment option, IPT may be a good fit for individuals whose eating disorder symptoms seem strongly associated with problematic relationships (Apple 1999).

With regard to eating disorders other than bulimia nervosa, a recent study among individuals who have binge eating disorder found that the group therapy formats for both CBT and IPT were equally effective at reducing binge eating, both when treatment ended and when evaluated one year later (Wilfley, et al. in press). Some therapists begin treatment of eating disorders with a structured CBT approach and then shift to an interpersonal focus if relationships appear to be difficult for the patient.

Your Ideas

Advantages: _____

_____

_____

Disadvantages: _____

_____

_____

Questions: _____

_____

_____

Feminist Therapy

This therapy can be conducted in an individual or family format. One goal is to examine the psychological development of the individual, both in the context of his or his personal and family relationships and the broader cultural environment. The guiding perspective of feminist therapy is that our society has different expectations for men and women. Specifically, for women there is an overemphasis on physical appearance and thinness. This type of treatment encourages people to challenge these cultural messages and empowers young women to have a clearer view of themselves as individuals.

Research support: At this time there has not been a lot of research to evaluate the effectiveness of this type of therapy; however, feminist therapy may play a valuable role in raising cultural awareness and increasing understanding of the sociopolitical factors involved in the development of eating disorders. This approach may be especially valuable for clients who have a history of physical or sexual abuse given that there are specific treatment principles designed to address this difficult issue (Garner and Needleman 1997).

Your Ideas

Advantages:_____

_____

_____

Disadvantages: _____

_____

_____

Questions: _____

_____

_____

Psychodynamic and Supportive Therapies

Psychodynamic therapy emphasizes the importance of examining past relationships in order to gain perspective on present relationships and their relation to eating symptoms. One goal is to gain insight about patterns in relationships with others, and how these relationships contribute to the person's view of him- or herself. Therapy focuses on analyzing motives that are unconscious or not immediately apparent. Questions may be raised, such as: what is motivating a person's self-starvation? What meaning does a person draw from his or her body? How have his or her needs been met in the past and in the present? Different forms of psychodynamic treatment vary in how much they focus on actively managing the eating disorder symptoms (i.e., binge eating and purging) versus how much they focus on the process of self-exploration.

In supportive therapy, the therapist's primary role is to help the individual identify problems and solutions for him or herself. The therapist listens carefully and reflects back what is heard in order to help the individual describe and clarify current problems. Rather than direct the client toward specific solutions or suggest certain strategies, the therapist encourages the client to come up with his or her own ideas to try. The client is considered responsible for making changes, and the role of the therapist is to facilitate, rather than direct, this change.

Research support: Although psychodynamic theories for eating disorders have been written about extensively and often inform how clinicians think about eating disorders, there has been little research to test the effectiveness of this form of therapy. In one study comparing a supportive approach to cognitive behavioral therapy, the CBT group decreased dieting behavior, and improved attitudes toward shape and weight, self-esteem, and mental health problems more than the supportive group did (Garner, et al. 1993), suggesting that CBT was a preferable first line of treatment.

Many people find psychodynamic approaches helpful; however, given that they have not yet been well tested for eating disorders, we generally recommend that they be considered after other treatment options have not been helpful. If your child's therapist provides psychodynamic treatment, it is reasonable to ask for the rationale supporting its use in your child's specific case.

Your Ideas

Advantages: _____

_____

_____

Disadvantages: _____

_____

_____

Questions: _____

_____

_____

Family Therapy

There are many different models of family therapy, but they share in common the view that understanding and changing an individual's illness is best done by examining the relations among family members and evaluating the roles that different family members play. The models vary in how directly they focus on the eating disorder symptoms and how directly they encourage parents to influence their child's eating. Frequently, there is a major emphasis placed on examining family interaction patterns and considering what patterns are healthy and how the eating disorder fits into the family's functioning as a whole.

Research support: Either a full course of family therapy, family therapy as an adjunct to individual therapy, or family consultations can be very valuable for young persons with an eating disorder (especially anorexia nervosa). In fact, once weight has been restored for a person with anorexia, family therapy has been found to be even more helpful than individual psychodynamic therapy if the anorexia nervosa started during childhood or adolescence (Dare, et al. 1995). Further, family therapy is usually one of the first recommended treatment choices for children and adolescents with anorexia nervosa who are still living at home (Dare and Eisler 2002).

Your Ideas

Advantages: _____

_____

_____

Disadvantages: _____

_____

_____

Questions: _____

_____

_____

Nutritional Counseling

Nutritional counseling frequently occurs along with psychotherapy and involves helping the client establish normal eating patterns. A nutritionist will help the young person develop healthier attitudes toward food and better ways to respond to hunger. In some treatment settings, the nutritional counselor will use aspects of cognitive behavioral therapy to examine unhealthy thoughts and beliefs about food. Consequently, it is worth asking potential counselors to describe their treatment plans; the focus on distorted attitudes about food may be helpful for your child, particularly if your child's psychotherapist is not addressing this.

Research support: Nutritional management is a helpful addition to many eating disorder treatments. Research supports the idea that nutritional management can lead to substantial improvement in eating disorder symptoms, including the reduction or elimination of binge eating (Laessle, et al. 1991). Having a nutritionist as a part of a treatment team can also give your child the specialized care she needs—allowing the nutritionist to help your child establish healthy eating patterns and the therapist to focus on your child's emotional and psychological health.

Your Ideas

Advantages: _____

_____

_____

Disadvantages: _____

_____

_____

Questions: _____

_____

_____

Inpatient Treatment

Hospital admission is more common with anorexia nervosa than with bulimia nervosa, but can happen whenever there are serious medical issues or concerns for safety. Inpatient treatment is typically one to two weeks, although it can be much longer depending on insurance coverage and the severity of medical complications and weight loss. The most common reasons for hospitalization include severe or rapid weight loss, lack of response to aggressive outpatient treatment, significant co-occurring mental health problems (such as depression, substance abuse, suicidal thoughts, or self-injurious behaviors), or serious medical complications.

Medical care and restoration to a healthier body weight are the highest priorities on an inpatient unit. The staff will typically teach strategies for developing normal eating and exercise habits, as well as ways to cope with stress and other emotional problems. Given that hospital stays are usually short in duration, an important component of care is establishing plans for aftercare and long-term treatment.

Research support: We view hospitalization as a critical step toward finding effective long-term care for severely ill persons, but it is not an end point of treatment. For people with bulimia nervosa, short-term hospitalization seems to be somewhat effective at disrupting the dangerous cycle of binge eating followed by purging. These positive changes can then be further established and maintained through outpatient therapy (Wiseman, et al. 2001).

For individuals with anorexia nervosa, short-term inpatient treatments do not seem to work as well, because the person does not usually have enough time to reach a sufficiently healthy weight (Wiseman, et al. 2001). As a consequence, hospital discharges that take place before an individual has gained sufficient weight are associated with higher relapse rates and negative treatment outcomes (Baran, Weltzon, and Kaye 1997). When hospitalization is needed, it is important to be a strong advocate for your child, and try to push your insurance company to approve a sufficient hospital stay.

The time needed at an inpatient facility varies depending on the rate of weight gain. Ideally, the child should be at 90 percent of his or her expected weight by the time of discharge with a typical weight gain of about two to three pounds a week (Garner and Needleman 1997). Although this can mean a long and expensive hospital stay, you can let your insurance company know that there is research evidence demonstrating that discharge before sufficient weight gain is not cost-effective because of the risk for rehospitalization. Of course, if steady weight gain is not occurring, it is reasonable to ask the inpatient program about this problem and to question the value of your child being in the hospital for a long period of time.

Your Ideas

Advantages: _____

_____

_____

Disadvantages: _____

_____

_____

Questions: _____

_____

_____

Medications

Medications for treating eating disorders have been advocated for over forty years, but determining their effectiveness remains a challenge.

Results vary across different research studies, depending on the problem being treated, the medication used, and other complicating diagnoses. Nonetheless, medications can play a very helpful role in recovery, particularly when used in conjunction with psychotherapy and nutritional rehabilitation, rather than alone (Garfinkel and Walsh 1997).

Some parents may be hesitant to have their child use medication, but we encourage you to be open minded and explore your child's options.

Research support. The research to date suggests that antidepressant medications can be helpful to many people with bulimia nervosa and some with anorexia nervosa (Walsh 2002). There is also some evidence that antidepressant medications may be helpful for individuals with binge eating disorder as well (Devlin 2002). The research on medication for eating disorders is expanding rapidly. The best approach is to consult with a knowledgeable and experienced psychiatrist who can help you determine the best course of treatment for your child. If your child's doctor does recommend medication, remember that finding a medication that works for any particular person can be a trial and error process. Try not to get discouraged if it takes a couple of tries to get the right medication for your child.

Your Ideas

Advantages: _____

_____

_____

Disadvantages: _____

_____

_____

Questions: _____

_____

_____

Criteria for Level of Care

Following your child's initial evaluation, a therapist will recommend a particular level of care, based on the severity of your child's symptoms and their degree of medical and psychiatric risk. The level of care can vary from the most intensive (hospitalization) to outpatient care. For a list of criteria typically used to determine level of care you might want to go to the Web site of the National Eating Disorders Association (NEDA 2001). It can give you a sense of what to expect.

Your Role in Treatment

Your relationship with your child's treatment team is an important one. Your level of involvement will depend on your child's age, your relationship with your child, and the severity of the disorder. But there are somethings you can expect to take place.

Reasonable Expectations

You should expect a treatment plan backed by research evidence supporting its effectiveness in treating eating disorders. We recommend that you discuss this treatment plan as soon as the evaluation is completed and that you talk with the therapist about a timeline when you can reevaluate the plan. This will help you give your child time and space and keep you from prematurely questioning whether this is the right therapist or form of treatment for your child. You may also want to ask how you can be most helpful. Although it is difficult to be patient and to trust that your child is receiving the care he or she needs, you should keep in mind that treatment is a gradual process without magic pills or quick fixes.

You can also request an initial family meeting to discuss what will happen in therapy, how each family member will be involved, a general sense of how long therapy will last, and what the realistic expectations for recovery are. Because your child may meet with the therapist without you present for most of the initial evaluation, you might want to talk with your child about your interest in being included in some way. Different therapists handle this differently, and your level of involvement may depend on your child's age, his or her desire to have you involved or not, and the severity of your child's symptoms. Some therapists meet directly with the parents. At the Yale Center for Eating and Weight Disorders, we have one therapist meet with the family and serve as the family consultant while another therapist serves as the child's primary caregiver. Regardless of your level of involvement, it is crucial that from the outset you, your child, and the therapist have a clear understanding about your role.

It is also reasonable to expect that the therapist will discuss confidentiality and its limits. This should be done during the first session and will help in determining your role and giving you a sense of how much information will be shared with you. If your child is a legal adult, you typically will not have access to information from therapy records or from the therapist. You should listen to your child and try to understand what he or she wants regarding your level of contact with the therapist. Keep in mind that there are alternatives to either hearing everything that happens in therapy or hearing nothing about what is discussed between your child and the therapist. There are many ways to establish helpful channels of communication, but the most important thing is for you to discuss your needs and to listen to your child's wishes if you want to set up an effective plan.

For all clients in a therapy setting, there are exceptions to confidentiality, and your child's therapist should review this. If a therapist learns that a client is planning to injure or kill him- or herself, this must be reported to people who can help ensure safety (by putting the child in the hospital or monitoring the child to make sure that no action is taken). Second, if a client indicates a plan to injure or kill someone else, that must be reported to the authorities. Third, if there is a report that abuse of a minor is occurring, the therapist is legally required to file a report to the local Department of Children and Families.

If your child is not a legal adult, you will have to give consent for treatment. This means that you will sign a form along with your child allowing him or her to participate in therapy. Although you legally have the right to access the information in your child's records, it is important to discuss this at the very beginning of treatment. It is usually beneficial for a child to be able to talk confidentially with a therapist without worrying that private, personal information is being shared with parents. On the other hand, as a parent, you may be worried and want to know how your child is doing. This is why it is vitally important to discuss confidentiality at the start of treatment and decide together what information will be shared with whom.

The Treatment Contract

It is reasonable to expect a clear treatment contract that addresses confidentiality and the limits of your contact with the therapist. Therapy can be set up so that everyone's expectations are recognized and addressed, and this involves clarifying what information (if any) will be shared with parents as well as when (or if) parents will have contact with the therapist. This will help prevent future misunderstandings and help facilitate a trusting relationship between your child and his or her therapist.

There are many ways to plan ahead to better meet everyone's needs, so here are a few ideas about possible ways to support your child's treatment:

- You could establish a system to receive regular feedback on how therapy is progressing. This might be especially helpful if your child's symptoms are severe. You may be able to arrange family meetings with the therapist at predetermined intervals (for example, on a monthly basis or every other month).

- For some families, it may be more helpful for treatment to be set up so that the child and therapist have complete confidentiality; the therapist does not have contact with the parents unless the child's safety is at risk. You, your child, and the therapist can determine ahead of time the definition of "at risk" which could include having suicidal thoughts, engaging in specific dangerous behaviors, reaching a critically low weight, or other difficulties that might require extra support.

- Your child's therapist might recommend or you might choose to pursue, family therapy with another therapist. In this type of treatment, everyone is together in the same room discussing ways to improve how people in your family interact with one other.

- Another option would be for you (and your partner) to consult with a professional who can offer guidance and support. Some parents benefit from meeting weekly or monthly to develop their parenting skills and to manage the challenges of helping a child who has an eating disorder. Other parents find it helpful to meet with a therapist on an as-needed basis, when they need assistance with more difficult problems.

- Parent support groups can be valuable resources for learning about eating disorders and developing ways to deal with your difficulties. It is always important for you to take care of yourself and have a place to voice your concerns!

Questions and Answers about What Happens in Treatment

Question: "How do I know if therapy is working? My daughter has been going to talk to this guy every week for three months. Shouldn't something be happening by now?"

Answer: This is a difficult question to answer. Different rates of change might be expected depending on the form of therapy and the nature and severity of your child's problems. Typically after three months, you would hope to see some behavioral changes, such as more balanced and regular eating, even though your child's attitudes toward food may still be unhealthy. A number of factors can complicate the rate of recovery, however. Anorexia nervosa usually takes longer to treat than bulimia or binge eating disorder, for example. In other cases, someone may be ambivalent about entering treatment or making changes; the initial phase of therapy may need to target the person's motivation and readiness to change before intensive eating disorder interventions can begin. (Of course, when medical complications are present, these need to be addressed immediately, regardless of the person's motivation). In addition, it is not uncommon for other psychological difficulties, such as depression or anxiety, to be present along with the eating disorder. These other difficulties may also need to be addressed if they interfere with treatment.

Given this high level of variability, we recommend that you ask your child's therapist at the outset of therapy what changes you can expect to see and when they will occur. The bottom line is that it is not realistic to have rigid expectations, but it is very reasonable to count on regular progress reports to make sure treatment is on track. If months have gone by and your child is not experiencing any improvement, it is acceptable to ask your child's therapist if he or she thinks another form of treatment might be more helpful.

Question: "I feel really embarrassed to go in for a family meeting, but my son's therapist wants to talk with me. I'm afraid the doctor is just going to make me feel like everything is my fault."

Answer: Family meetings can be a critical part of the recovery process, but they should never be a shaming or blaming experience. The goal is to work together to develop solutions to family problems and to find creative ways to help your family function most effectively and support your child's recovery. You might want to let the therapist know your concerns in advance of the meeting so that he or she can be sensitive to your needs. However, you should also try to be positive about your role. If the therapist suggests a change, do not take it as criticism. You can play a positive role in the recovery process without assuming that you are responsible for the initial problem.

Keep in mind that the therapist wants to work with you—not alienate you—so these meetings are generally very constructive and supportive. Family meetings are often very emotional, but they should leave you feeling hopeful that recovery is possible and that you can work together toward a common goal.

Question: "It seems that each time my son goes to the therapist, he comes back more moody and depressed than before. Is it normal for him to be feeling this way while he is in treatment?"

Answer: Therapy can be a challenging and emotionally draining process because your son is being pushed to change his behaviors in ways that can feel very scary at first, and because he is being encouraged to talk about feelings and thoughts that he may find difficult and painful to express. Try to be understanding and supportive if your son seems a little moodier than usual as he adjusts to a new, healthier way of functioning. However, if you feel that your child is becoming unusually depressed, do not ignore it; he may need additional help. Talk to your son and then the therapist if you are worried that he is in trouble.

Question: "What do I do if my daughter drops out of treatment?"

Answer: Try to be patient and understanding. You can help motivate her to return to treatment, but ultimately it will have to be her choice, since forcing her would probably not be effective. Try to present alternative resources, and be open to discussing her thoughts on reentering therapy or trying another approach. (If you feel that your daughter's health is in immediate danger, contact her medical doctor about your concerns.)

Question: "I know my daughter is supposed to be filling out these food records, but I see them sit on the counter all week, and then she fills them all out in the car on the way to therapy. I don't even think she fills in everything she really ate. Should I say something to her therapist?"

Answer: It is frustrating to see your child not using one of the therapy tools, or worse, not being truthful with her therapist. When it comes to food records, however, sometimes it takes a while for people to overcome the shame they feel about their eating and be completely truthful in their records. You could open up the topic by just asking her what she thinks about keeping food records. Alternatively, you could tell both your daughter and her therapist that you have a concern about treatment and you would like a few minutes at the beginning of a session to join them and discuss it. If this is not acceptable to them, you could ask for the name of a family therapist and ask to have a session with your daughter to discuss your concern that your daughter is not being honest with her own therapist.

Question: "I know my own child, and I can tell you that all of her problems with eating started when she began seeing this new boyfriend last summer. He is a bad influence on her and she has changed a lot since seeing him. I want to call up the therapist and tell her this, but I don't want her to tell my daughter that I called. Can I make a confidential call to my child's therapist?

Answer: Confidentiality applies to the patient, not the parent. If you do call your daughter's therapist, it is likely that she will tell your daughter that you called and what you said. If there is something important that you want the therapist to know, it would make sense to set up a time to talk with the therapist with your child in the room. You may be afraid that this will make your daughter angry, but if you are really worried about the influence of her boyfriend, there is no sense in trying to keep those concerns a secret. An open, honest discussion of your observations and worries, perhaps facilitated by a professional, may help improve communication between you and your daughter.

Question: "If the eating disorder isn't my fault, why do I have to be such a big part of the recovery? It sounds like this is my daughter's problem, not mine."

Answer: Each family needs to figure out what is right for them, but whenever family members can work collaboratively, the likelihood of a positive outcome is increased. This is especially true for younger children with eating problems, who most need family structure and support.

For older adolescents and young adults, there are benefits when a family works together to create a home environment that makes recovery easier. Thus, even if the family does not feel comfortable seeking treatment together, it can still be valuable to speak to the child's therapist to find out what you can do at home.

Karen's Story

Karen was a nineteen-year-old college student when her parents pleaded with her to get help for an eating disorder. Karen's weight had been dropping steadily for several months, and her parents noticed that she was eating very infrequently. Although she didn't think that she needed help, Karen met with a psychologist because she felt guilty about causing her parents to worry about her. Karen's evaluation resulted in a diagnosis of anorexia nervosa and the following recommendations: weekly outpatient therapy, weekly appointments with a nutritionist, a physical exam, and frequent medical visits with a physician.

Although not convinced that she had a problem requiring so many appointments, Karen reluctantly agreed to have a physical exam and to meet with a nutritionist for a consultation. Her doctor's appointment confirmed that her weight was below normal, but her vital signs and lab results were in the normal range, indicating that she was not acutely at risk. Even though she was medically stable at that time, her low weight and ongoing restriction of food prompted her physician to recommend monthly medical visits to monitor her physical health. Karen was not yet at the point where hospitalization or a day-treatment program would be recommended, but both her physician and her psychologist expressed the importance of regularly assessing her need for an increased level of care.

Still uncertain why everyone was making such a fuss about her eating habits, Karen also started to meet with a nutritionist and was surprised to hear that she wouldn't be forced to eat huge meals every day. She and the nutritionist developed a plan together that seemed reasonable, and Karen felt relieved that she wasn't going to be pressured into eating too much.

Karen was also somewhat relieved about the appointments with her psychologist. She had been worried that she was going to be told something terrible at the end of the evaluation, like she was crazy or a bad person, and she didn't want her parents hearing about any of the personal things that she told the psychologist. During the first appointment, Karen was happy to hear that anything discussed would be confidential unless her own or another person's safety was at risk. Also, she was very relieved to know that her parents would not receive information from the evaluation or from future appointments without her written consent, because she was legally an adult.

Meanwhile, Karen's parents were very concerned about her health and interested in knowing more about her status from the professionals meeting with her. Karen, however, wanted her treatment to be private, and although she wanted to ease her parents' worries, she also wanted them to trust her and not feel like they had to get information from anyone else. She and her therapist discussed this dilemma and decided together that they would meet with her parents for a session to review the treatment plan, diagnosis, and goals, and they determined ahead of time specifically which issues Karen felt comfortable sharing with them.

Karen's parents were happy to hear that they would be included in a session and they were especially relieved to learn that their daughter would be continuing with treatment. The family meeting was very educational for them. They listened to both the therapist and their daughter talk about anorexia, Karen's particular symptoms, the plan for medical and nutrition appointments, and the goals for therapy. They understood the importance of Karen's treatment being confidential and asked how they could be helpful in supporting her recovery. Karen asked them to stop inquiring about her eating every day, and her parents expressed that they would be able to be less intrusive if she could let them know how she was doing once a week. The therapist recommended that their family check-ins focus more on her feelings, and also that Karen and her parents discuss activities other than eating. Now that Karen was being seen regularly by a treatment team, she and her parents would be able to resume talking about other events and experiences, focus less on her eating habits, and trust that her health was being addressed.

Patty's Story

During her annual physical exam, Patty, a fourteen-year-old high school student, admitted that recently she'd been feeling light-headed, dizzy, tired, and cold. She was also having trouble concentrating and remembering things, and the physical exam revealed unstable vital signs and very low weight. Patty also acknowledged that she had been limiting her eating, exercising for hours every day, and vomiting several times a day. After talking with her about eating disorders and their serious consequences, Patty's doctor recommended that she be admitted to an inpatient hospitalization program until she was more stable medically.

Patty was terrified about going to the hospital, and her mother was shocked to hear that her daughter's health was at risk. The six-day hospitalization focused on improving Patty's nutrition, rehydrating her with plenty of fluids, and establishing follow-up treatment. Once her vital signs and labs were within the normal range, Patty was discharged to an eating disorders day-treatment program where she participated in groups, learned about the causes and treatment of eating disorders, and attended therapy sessions, both individually and with her family. During the six-week program, Patty struggled to understand how she had come to develop an eating disorder and developed ways to combat urges to restrict and purge. Her parents and brother attended a support group for families and identified ways to support Patty in her recovery. An important part of this program was setting up outpatient treatment, and the staff helped Patty find a therapist who specialized in eating disorders. They also recommended that Patty's family continue with family therapy, which the family agreed to do.

Upon discharge from day treatment, Patty and her family met regularly with their outpatient therapists. Because of Patty's young age and recently severe symptoms, her parents requested that they meet at least monthly with Patty and her therapist to discuss progress and problems. They did not want to interfere with Patty's treatment or intrude on her private interactions with her therapist, but they were concerned about her health and wanted to be included in this way. Patty agreed and was relieved that her parents wanted to help her and take time out of their schedules to attend appointments with her. Meanwhile, the family also met together with their family therapist twice a month to improve their relationships and learn ways to talk more openly with each other about difficulties.

Lynn's Story

Lynn was twenty years old, lived at home, and worked in retail as a salesperson. Having suffered with bulimia for four years, she decided that she wanted to end the constant cycle of bingeing and purging, and she made an appointment with a therapist for an evaluation. Cognitive behavioral therapy was recommended, and Lynn learned that this would entail establishing more regular eating (not skipping meals, having three meals and three snacks a day), writing down what she ate (keeping food records), challenging distorted thoughts about food and appearance, and developing healthier ways of expressing feelings. Part of therapy would also involve understanding and improving the ways she relates to others; Lynn found herself having to deal with this issue right away.

Lynn's mother wanted to be involved in her treatment. She told Lynn that she wanted to meet with her therapist and that she needed to know how to manage difficulties at home, especially what to do when Lynn was vomiting in the bathroom. Lynn did not want her mother involved in her treatment for a number of reasons, however. First, she did not want her therapy sessions to turn into "tattling sessions" in which her mother would list all of the things Lynn had done wrong. She also liked her therapist a lot and was worried about hearing her mother's opinion; Lynn had always felt swayed by her mother's opinions and didn't want to risk being swayed in a negative way in this situation. She also did not feel ready to talk openly with her mother about these feelings but acknowledged that making improvements in communicating more directly with her mother would be a treatment goal.

Lynn and her therapist decided that including her mother at this point might not be helpful. Lynn's mother was disappointed, but she was able to understand that it might be useful for her to seek help and support elsewhere for her questions and concerns. Lynn's therapist provided referral information, and her mother started to meet with another therapist, who helped her develop strategies for managing problems in the home.

Creating Solutions

This section is to help you most effectively facilitate your child's recovery in therapy. There are a number of challenges that you can expect to encounter, so thinking about these issues in advance can help you avoid arguments and misunderstandings later. All family members will likely need to make compromises at different times. We raise some questions and provide some guidelines to help you establish a family contract to make therapy work more smoothly, to think through issues of confidentiality, and to plan how to deal with disagreements between you and your child.

Planning for Treatment

Much of the confusion that arises at the outset of therapy relates to different expectations from you, your child, and the therapist. There are a number of planning issues that need to be worked out so that everyone knows what to expect. Here are some practical things that should be clarified at the beginning of treatment.

1. Cost of each session: _____

2. Length of each session: _____

3. Cancellation policy: _____
   (Many therapists have a twenty-four-hour cancellation policy, where you must cancel with twenty-four hours notice to avoid being charged.)

4. Time of scheduled session: _____
   (Try to schedule sessions at a time that will minimize disruption of work and school so that you can avoid any difficulty coming to the sessions. Also, try to have a backup person who can drive your child to the session if you cannot.)

5. Frequency of sessions: _____
   (Clients usually meet with the therapist once a week, but this can vary based on the needs of the client.)

Confidentiality

As we discussed earlier, the limits of confidentiality are important to clarify when a child is in treatment. The therapist should clarify and answer any questions you or your child may have. It can also be helpful to address the following questions (often jointly with your child and the therapist) to come up with a solution that works for your family.

1. Who is responsible for getting the child to the sessions? What is the backup plan?

2. If the child misses a session without the parent's knowledge, does the therapist have the child's permission to notify the parent? If not, does the child agree to tell the parent?

3. Who will be monitoring the child's medical status? Will this information be given directly to the parents or to the child? Can the parents request information directly from the doctor?

4. How will the therapist track changes in symptoms over time? How will this information be given to the parents?

5. What should the parents do if they have information they want to share with the therapist?

6. Can the parents ask the child how the session went each week? Or, should they wait for the child to share information?

7. Can the parents ask the therapist how the session went each week? If not, how will the parents be notified of how things are going?

Write down some other questions you want to address:

_____

_____

_____

What If You and Your Child Disagree?

It is not unusual for parents and their children to disagree about the best course of action in treatment. We will illustrate this situation with a case example.

Helen's Story

Helen was a twelve-year-old middle school student. After discovering a box a laxatives in Helen's drawer, Helen's mother brought her daughter to a therapist. In the first meeting, it was clear that Helen did not want her mother included in her therapy at all—she said that it was her problem and she wanted to fix it, and she really didn't want her mother's help. In fact, Helen argued that if her mother were involved it would just make things worse because her mother would try to take over and control everything. The therapist, Helen, and her mother agreed that Helen would have weekly sessions and her mother would not ask how the sessions went or comment on her eating during the week. At the same time, her mother did have the right to talk to Helen's pediatrician and find out her weight and the results of medical tests. The mother decided that if she could keep track of Helen's medical status (and as long as that status continued to improve), she would not try to influence Helen's eating or ask her questions about her therapy sessions.

They planned that after four weeks, Helen, her mother, and the therapist would have a meeting to discuss how they each felt things were going. Helen's mother was given the name of another therapist to contact if she wanted to talk about the situation from her own perspective. Helen and her therapist met weekly and Helen appreciated the break from her mother's constant questioning about her eating. Helen's mother respected Helen's desire to have a private relationship with her therapist, and Helen's symptoms continued to improve.

There were times, however, when Helen's mother wanted to discuss certain food related decisions with her. For example, Helen wanted to go to a summer camp that specialized in outdoor camping and mountain climbing, and her mother worried that this would be too much exercise and would leave too few food choices for her. Rather than get into fights about this at home, Helen and her mother went to one of Helen's therapy sessions to discuss the camp and her concerns. The therapist facilitated a discussion between Helen and her mother about the pros and cons of going to the camp, and in the end, Helen decided to wait one more year before trying this camp.

If you are having disagreements over treatment with your child, it may be useful to learn how to compromise. In the following exercise, describe some disagreements you have had, and list what you would like, what your child would like, and then develop a compromise solution that hopefully considers both sides. If there are other decision makers involved, such as siblings, you can add another section to take their unique wishes and concerns into account.

Topic: What to do about missed therapy sessions

Parents' wishes: _____

Child's wishes: _____

Possible solution: _____

Topic: What to do if eating disorder symptoms are getting worse

Parents' wishes: _____

Child's wishes: _____

Possible solution: _____

Topic: Who should get to see and comment on food records

Parents' wishes: _____

Child's wishes: _____

Possible solution: _____

Topic: What are the main goals in therapy

Parents' wishes: _____

Child's wishes: _____

Possible solution: _____

Now come up with your own topics that are specific to your family's concerns:

Topic: _____

Parents' wishes: _____

Child's wishes: _____

Possible solution: _____

Topic: _____

Parents' wishes: _____

Child's wishes: _____

Possible solution: _____

Topic: _____

Parents' wishes: _____

Child's wishes: _____

Possible solution: _____

Terms I Want to Clarify

As you learn about eating disorders and treatment, we suggest that you keep track of terms that you want to clarify. You can jot them down here, and then ask a health care professional for an explanation. The treatment process should not be mysterious. You have a right to understand what is happening to your child and your family.

Term	Definition
_____	_____
_____	_____
_____	_____
_____	_____

CHAPTER 7

What about Special Cases?
Specific Groups and Co-occurring Problems

When we were told that our son, Jack, had an eating disorder, we were shocked. Sure, I'd heard of eating disorders, but it never occurred to me that I needed to worry about my athletic, six-foot-tall son getting one. He felt embarrassed that he had a "girl's problem," and that made it even harder to get him to seek help. We were relieved to learn that he was not the only teenage boy with this problem.

—Jeanne, mother of seventeen-year-old boy
with bulimia nervosa

People familiar with eating disorders may try to tell you about the "typical" individual with anorexia nervosa or bulimia nervosa, but the truth is that every person is unique. While the symptoms may seem easy to predict, the reasons why each person develops these symptoms are specific to that individual. It takes time to reflect upon each person's story to understand the different aspects of his or her experience.

The aim of this chapter is to address circumstances apart from the eating disorder that may be relevant for your child. Some of you are parents of male children who have eating disorders. Others of you may have a child who has another medical diagnosis, such as diabetes or obesity. Sometimes children with eating disorders have a second psychiatric diagnosis, such as depression, anxiety, or a history of trauma. These children may require additional treatment considerations. This chapter will also address information available on eating disorders in different ethnic groups, very young children, athletes, and bodybuilders.

Debunking Myths about Special Populations

Myth: Boys don't get real eating disorders—it's something different.

Research says: Eating disorders among males are just as real and serious as they are among females. A community-based study of anorexia nervosa and bulimia nervosa found that one out of about every seven people reporting an eating disorder is male (Andersen 2002). Sadly, eating disorders are often misdiagnosed in males because many males only seek help under the guise of another medical problem, such as endocrine or gastrointestinal difficulties. This can make it more difficult for doctors to recognize the eating disorder.

Myth: The more athletes exercise, the better their performance will be.

Research says: Excessive exercising and restricted eating can have severe consequences for athletes. It is now well established that certain types of sports and activities that demand control over weight for reasons of performance or appearance (such as ballet, long-distance running, and figure skating) are risk factors for eating disorders (Byrne 2002). Athletes often have personality factors typically seen in individuals suffering from eating disorders, including perfectionism, competitiveness, and a high achievement orientation (Byrne 2002).

Still, there seem to be important differences between athletes and persons with eating disorders who are not athletic. For example, athletes with eating disorders have better self-images, report feeling less dissatisfied with their bodies, and may not suffer from depression as much as nonathletes (Byrne 2002). The motivation for weight control may also differ—athletes may experience pressure to lose weight for better performance, rather than simply to become thinner (Byrne 2002).

Special Issues for Different Populations

Here, we will provide some background information on conditions that commonly co-occur with eating disorders. If you have a question about an issue that makes your child's eating disorder unique, you should raise it with your child's doctor and/or therapist.

Co-occurring Medical Conditions

Having a child with a serious medical condition and caring for a child with an eating disorder raise many of the same challenging questions. When your child is struggling with both of these problems, it can feel overwhelming to keep track of all of his or her medical needs.

Parents need to be aware that their children can abuse features of their illness or its treatment to promote weight loss. These behaviors are especially dangerous, as they exacerbate the original condition as well as introduce the risks of weight loss. Sometimes an eating disorder may develop in response to a medical condition, where there is a focus on food for medical management of the illness. Sometimes an eating disorder may develop as a way of managing the painful emotions associated with a serious medical problem. If you suspect your child is engaging in these types of behaviors, consulting with a medical professional is extremely important.

Diabetes and Eating Disorders

Incorrect use of insulin and binge eating can contribute to poor diabetic control. Research indicates that diabetics who have an eating disorder are more likely to have both short- and long-term medical complications than diabetics without an eating disorder. Not surprisingly, persons with both anorexia nervosa and insulin-dependent diabetes mellitus will almost invariably require hospitalization to restore weight and normalize eating. If your child has diabetes and an eating disorder, there is an important need for medical attention and nutritional counseling (Powers 1997).

We suggest that you initially monitor blood sugar levels closely to ensure that your child is not reporting false levels. While it is difficult to question your child, this is a situation where your child's medical well-being is at stake, and you need to make sure that your child is not in physical danger. You will need to monitor blood sugar levels throughout recovery because insulin requirements may change as weight is gained or binge eating stops.

You can educate your child about the relationship between eating disorders and diabetes. For example, because insulin requirements can decrease with weight loss, some people may think they can stop being diabetic if they become thin enough. This belief can be dangerous, and education helps in this regard. Similarly, it is important to help young persons distinguish between the healthy monitoring of their eating (necessary for appropriate diabetic control) from the obsessive restriction of foods (associated with eating disorders). Detailed nutritional management for diabetes can inadvertently lead to the preoccupation with food that is common to eating problems.

Obesity and Eating Disorders

There has long been debate about whether obesity should be considered an eating disorder. We think about obesity as a health condition that is caused by a series of complex variables including genetic, environmental, psychological, physiological, metabolic, and sociocultural factors. Regardless of your position on this debate, obesity frequently co-occurs with binge eating disorder so it deserves special mention here.

The medical definitions of obesity have changed over the years. Currently, the most common way of assessing obesity is with a value called the body mass index (BMI). The formula for BMI is weight in kilograms divided by height in meters squared (kg/m^2). An easy way to do this is to take weight in pounds and divide it by height in inches, then divide again by height in inches, and multiply by 703. The current guidelines suggest that a BMI over 25 indicates the person is overweight, and a BMI over 30 indicates the person is obese. It is important to consider these numbers in the context of the individual's overall health and fitness level. For example, some athletes have significant muscle mass, making them technically overweight, even though their health may be excellent despite the number of pounds on the scale.

In general, however, being obese is associated with significant health risks and is a highly stigmatized condition. There is evidence that overweight individuals are discriminated against in a variety of settings, including education, employment, health care, and relationships. This is becoming a more pressing social issue as the rates of obesity are rising steadily, particularly among children.

Many people who have binge eating disorder are also obese, but all obese individuals do not have binge eating disorder. Typically, people with binge eating disorder seek treatment for obesity, rather than for the eating disorder (Marcus 1997). In fact, a study done at a university clinic found that nearly 30 percent of patients receiving obesity treatment also met criteria for binge eating disorder (Spitzer, et al. 1993). It seems that some people begin binge eating following their first diet, while other people start binge eating first and then diet later as a response to the weight gain.

There is an important relationship between weight and binge eating, with more negative psychological consequences occurring for the overweight person if he or she binge eats. For example, research has found that as people have more severe problems with binge eating, it is linked to higher feelings of ineffectiveness, stronger perfectionist attitudes, more impulsivity, and lower self-esteem (De Zwaan, et al. 1994). Binge eating, rather than being overweight alone, seems to cause psychological difficulties. One study found that 60 percent of obese persons who binge eat had a co-occurring psychiatric disorder compared to 28 percent of obese persons who do not binge (Marcus, et al. 1990).

Special Considerations

If you have an obese child, it is important to work to protect his or her self-esteem and sense of pride in his or her body. As we mentioned, our society can be very prejudiced against overweight people, so you should try to help your child cope with the stigma of obesity. Take opportunities to make it clear that you are primarily interested in your child's health. You want your child to enjoy physical activity and pay attention to what his or her body can do, rather than focus on what his or her body looks like.

You can emphasize good health by modeling healthy eating and exercise behaviors. Due to biological and social factors, children of heavy parents are more likely to be heavy than children of thin parents. You can set an example by eating well yourself, and not using food to meet emotional needs. When family members offer comfort in the form of food, a young person may learn to use eating as a way to cope with negative emotions. Try to incorporate physical activity into the time you spend with your child. Eating well and enjoying physical activities are important goals for the whole family—not just the overweight child. (See chapter 5.)

As with any eating disorder, you should check with your doctor about your child's physical condition. Health risks related to obesity include hypertension (high blood pressure), diabetes, cardiovascular disease, some forms of cancer, endocrine problems, gall bladder disease, lung and breathing problems, arthritis, and sleep disturbances. We do not want to alarm you; the vast majority of these health risks occur in adulthood, but it is never too early to care for your body. Exercise goes a long way toward reducing the risk of disease, even if a person remains overweight.

Finally, we encourage you to be wary if your child wants to try a drastic weight loss measure. Over-the-counter weight loss medications are at best, ineffective, and at worst, unsafe. You should also talk seriously with a doctor you trust before considering a prescription weight loss medication. There are no magic solutions to the problem of obesity, but parents can help their children distinguish between healthy weight loss methods and unsafe ones.

Eating Disorders that Occur before Puberty

This book has centered on the treatment of young people with eating disorders, but most of our recommendations are for parents of adolescent children. When caring for a prepubescent child with an eating disorder, there are some critical developmental issues to consider. The following types of eating disorders are seen most frequently among prepubescent children:

Anorexia nervosa does occur among young children. These children report the same types of thoughts as seen in older children and adults with the illness, such as a fear of fat even though they are underweight, and fear of weight gain. Interestingly, among young children with anorexia, a larger proportion are boys (approximately 20 to 25 percent of referrals) relative to the gender distribution in older populations (Bryant-Waugh and Lask 2002). It is not known why this gender difference exists for different ages.

Food avoidance emotional disorder is thought of as a partial syndrome of anorexia nervosa (Bryant-Waugh and Lask 2002). Children who have this disorder will avoid food in general, but do not have the full symptoms of anorexia. The chances for recovery are good. Children with this problem often experience anxiety and depression and dislike school.

Selective eating occurs when children eat a very narrow range of foods. Typically, children may eat only three or four different foods which may not provide them with the nutrients they need. Despite their restricted diet, many of these children experience normal growth but may have social difficulties. You should consult with your pediatrician to determine if your child needs specialized treatment for selective eating (Bryant-Waugh and Lask 2002).

Pervasive refusal syndrome is a serious condition and can be life threatening. Children with this disorder usually see a doctor for symptoms of anorexia nervosa; however, when forced feeding is begun, the child's condition tends to get worse. Children suffering from this syndrome will often refuse to eat, drink, walk, talk, or engage in self-care. Some researchers feel that this eating problem may be associated with post-traumatic stress disorder (Lask and Bryant-Waugh 1997).

We did not mention bulimia nervosa in this list because it is very rare among young children. We also left out other feeding problems that are not considered eating disorders. For example, *pica* is an illness in which a person repeatedly eats nonedible substances, like wall plaster, clay, paint, wool, ashes, and earth. Although tasting or mouthing of strange objects is normal in infants and toddlers, if the habit persists after two years of age, it should be evaluated.

Special Considerations

Physical complications among prepubescent children with eating disorders are of particular concern. Eating disorders at such a young age can interfere with normal growth and development. It is critical to begin an intensive and comprehensive treatment program as soon as you can.

What should your role be? You will probably need to take a more directive role in ensuring your young child's health than you would with an adolescent. The idea is not to control all aspects of your child's world but to take charge of eating and safety issues until your child is headed toward recovery. This can be a very challenging task because your child will not want to give you that control. However, your child needs to be under the care of adults who can guarantee her or his health.

One of the more painful things you may have to do as a parent of a young person with anorexia or pervasive refusal is support your child during refeeding. Refeeding is common in pediatrics because younger children cannot adequately care for themselves. Refeeding is typically done at the hospital using a nasogastric tube, although some pediatricians prefer intravenous feeding. Your child may find this forced feeding very anxiety provoking, but it is essential to his or her health and recovery.

Once your child no longer needs artificial refeeding, he or she can start eating again. This usually begins at the hospital, but may be continued by you at home. You will need to follow the guidelines given by your child's caregivers.

Co-occurring Psychological Problems

We recognize that handling an eating disorder is challenging on its own, so it can be especially exasperating when your child also has an additional psychological problem. Unfortunately, it is all too common. Comorbidity refers to the occurrence of more than one problem. Many researchers have found high rates of psychiatric comorbidity among people suffering from eating disorders (Bulik 2002). The most frequent ones are: depression, anxiety, substance abuse (drugs or alcohol), and obsessive-compulsive symptoms. These problems can be exacerbated by malnutrition and unhealthy eating behaviors. At the same time, the eating disorder symptoms can be made worse by the stress and negative mood associated with other psychological problems. Thus, the combination of the problems can make each problem worse.

Depending on the severity of the different problems, your child's therapist will determine how to focus treatment. Sometimes a person will see an eating disorder specialist as well as another specialized therapist. When psychological problems occur as a consequence of eating problems, treatment of the eating disorder may be sufficient to resolve both areas of difficulty. Questions regarding the order and scope of treatment will depend on the onset and severity of the different psychological problems and how the person responds to treatment initially.

Researchers do not know for sure whether psychological disorders simply co-occur in certain individuals with eating disorders, or whether one disorder causes another. The relationships between eating disorders and other problems can vary depending upon the psychological disorder. We have summarized some of the relationships below:

Depression and Other Mood Disorders

Depression refers to a pervasive feeling of sadness or irritability, which is often accompanied by feelings of hopelessness, poor concentration, low energy, difficulties sleeping and eating, and lack of interest in activities. Other mood or affective disorders include bipolar disorder (where a person swings between feeling depressed and having a very high, elevated, or manic mood) and dysthymia (a long-lasting, lower-level depression).

Research suggests that people with eating disorders are at very high risk of experiencing depression at some point in their lives (Braun, et al.

1994). There are excellent treatments available for depression, and we strongly recommend that you do not ignore this problem. If the depression is occurring as a consequence of your child's eating disorder, his or her mood problems may not require special treatment. Your child's mood may improve as the eating disorder improves, but this should be monitored closely by a professional. If you suspect your child has severe depression, including suicidal thoughts, professional help is crucial.

Substance Abuse

It has been well established that a significant portion of people with eating disorders also abuse drugs or alcohol. It seems that people with bulimia nervosa are more likely than people with anorexia nervosa to have problems with substance abuse (Holderness, Brooks-Gunn, and Warren 1994).

There are a number of possible explanations for the link between eating disorders and substance use. One possibility is that some people have an "addictive personality," and tend to do all sorts of things compulsively, which would include binge eating and abusing drugs and alcohol. Another possibility is that a person with an eating disorder feels a lot of emotional pain and may use drugs or alcohol to self-medicate to relieve that pain. It is also possible that there are genetic factors that contribute to the development of both eating disorders and substance use.

Why this problem is happening may be less important than how you handle it. Unfortunately, if your child is actively using drugs and alcohol, he or she may be less responsive to eating disorders treatment. Given the addictive nature of drugs, your child is likely to need help to stop abusing these substances. You may want to ask a therapist about specialized treatment at an addictions treatment center or consider Alcoholics or Narcotics Anonymous meetings in your area. In terms of treating both substance abuse and eating disorders, it is very difficult to engage anyone in treatment for an eating disorder if he or she is still using drugs and alcohol. Your role, as always, is to be supportive of your child as a person but to be firm about the fact that these dangerous behaviors are unacceptable.

Anxiety Disorders

There are many different kinds of anxiety disorders. In panic disorder, people experience intense, sudden feelings of fear, accompanied by symptoms such as sweating, dizziness, difficulty breathing, and accelerated heart rate. In generalized anxiety disorder, people worry excessively that terrible things may happen. In social phobia, people fear social or performance situations, such as public speaking or dating. Other phobias are targeted toward specific things, such as fear of flying, snakes, heights, closed spaces, and so on. In post-traumatic stress disorder (PTSD), people experience recurrent memories and anxiety related to a past trauma, such as being raped or seeing someone killed. In obsessive-compulsive disorder (OCD), people experience repeated intrusive, unwanted thoughts or feel compelled to repeat a certain action, such as checking that the door is locked or washing their hands.

When anxiety disorders and eating disorders co-occur, it is not always clear that one disorder has directly caused the other. For example, obsessive-compulsive characteristics, such as perfectionism and a rigid focus on detail, are consistent with the behaviors and thoughts of people with anorexia nervosa. Fortunately, there are well researched treatments for many of the anxiety disorders. Again, we recommend seeing a therapist who specializes in this area.

Victims of Sexual Abuse

Post-traumatic stress disorder can be due to a history of sexual abuse. Though the exact relationship between childhood sexual abuse and disordered eating is still being studied, research suggests that sexual abuse is not a "specific" risk factor for an eating disorder (Fallon and Wonderlich 1997). This means that if your child experiences eating problems, you should not assume that he or she has been sexually abused. At the same time, try to be a nonjudgmental and compassionate listener if your child wants to talk about a painful experience.

Children who do experience sexual trauma may or not develop later psychiatric problems. The research suggests that the degree of psychiatric difficulty following trauma relates to a number of factors, including the vulnerability of the child at the time of abuse, the type and degree of abuse, and the reactions of the child and family to the abuse (Vanderlinden and Vandereycken 1996).

There are different theories on how sexual trauma can lead to the development of an eating disorder. One theory is that sexual trauma can make a person feel ashamed of his or her body and feel a sense of loathing toward it. Negative feelings about one's body can make a person more vulnerable to an eating disorder (Tripp and Petrie 2001). Other researchers have thought that disordered eating may develop as a way of escaping the strong emotions that are associated with the trauma (Schwartz and Gay 1996). Still others believe that individuals cope with trauma by engaging in an array of impulsive self-destructive behaviors that include eating disorders (Wonderlich, et al. 2001).

Dealing with the consequences of abuse can be extremely painful for parents. If your child has been a victim of abuse, it will be important for you to ensure that your home is a safe environment. Supporting your child at this time might include being aware of his or her emotional difficulties and providing attention, concern, and understanding.

Sometimes children who have an eating disorder and have been abused engage in self-destructive behaviors, such as stealing, drug or alcohol use, and promiscuity. When these behaviors occur, they are naturally very upsetting. People engage in these harmful behaviors because they are in pain. If your child is hurting him or herself, it is a cry for help. This behavior does not mean that your child is a bad person or intentionally wants to hurt you or other family members. Try to be supportive of your child even as you communicate that these behaviors are unacceptable. Help your child seek professional guidance to learn healthier ways of coping with painful feelings.

Special Considerations

There are some unique challenges in treating a young person who has an eating disorder and a trauma history. Many of the challenges come from the need to address post-traumatic stress reactions in addition to the eating problem. Whether the trauma and the eating should be addressed simultaneously or in sequence will depend on the urgency of the care required for the eating disorder and the extent that the child is willing to talk about the abuse. This is an issue that you will want to discuss with your child's therapist.

If your child has developed PTSD, it may be important for treatment to focus on managing these symptoms. This will involve educating the person about common symptoms of trauma, learning to tolerate intense feelings, and developing adaptive ways of thinking about the trauma. There are a number of common physical and psychological effects of childhood sexual abuse, and knowing what to expect can make a person feel less crazy and out of control.

What can you do at home? Perhaps the biggest challenge for you as a parent is to be patient—the treatment for an eating disorder and PTSD can be a long and bumpy road. There may be a lot of acting out at home or moodiness in response to the distress caused by dealing with these issues in therapy. Your understanding and support are critical. The other role that you can play is creating a safe place for your child to talk about what happened.

Regardless of whether the abuse happened at home or not, with a family member or by another person, we hope that you will do everything possible to insure that your home is now a safe place for your child. This means doing whatever is necessary to insure that abuse will not re-occur in the home. If this is a relevant concern for your family, we recommend that you contact your local child and family services organization for help.

Males with Eating Disorders

It is a myth that only young women get eating disorders. In fact, the number of men who develop an eating problem seems to be on the rise. As we noted earlier, there are many similarities in the nature and treatment of eating disorders for males and females. There are some meaningful differences, however, that can be helpful for you to understand as a parent. For example, boys with eating problems are more likely than girls to be involved in a sport where weight control influences performance (Braun, et al. 1999). While girls and women tend to be hyperfocused on weight, boys and men tend to be more concerned about shape. Consequently, the reasons men and women diet are sometimes different. Boys typically diet to avoid being teased about their weight or to increase sports performance (Andersen 1999).

Excessive exercise may be a warning sign that your son has an eating disorder. Young men who want to lose weight are more likely to use exercise than a restrictive diet (Drewnowski and Yee 1987). An evaluation of magazines targeted at females found a greater number of articles and advertisements geared toward weight reduction, whereas the magazines targeted at males included more articles related to shape and fitness (Andersen and DiDomencio 1992).

There are some differences between the care that boys and girls with eating disorders receive. In one review, females were found to receive more days of inpatient treatment than males (Striegel-Moore, et al. 2000). Another study found that some inpatient treatment centers lack gender-specific facilities or refuse to admit males altogether (Andersen 2002). It is unclear why this discrepancy occurs. Be an advocate for your son and ask for the care he needs.

A common stereotype is that males with eating disorders are gay. Most males with eating disorders are not homosexual, but it does seem that there is a higher percentage of males with eating disorder among homosexual males than among heterosexual males (Andersen 2002). Although no one knows exactly why this is the case, one possibility is that thinness is valued highly in the gay male community (Andersen 1999). Research among British males found that homosexual males reported more eating disturbances and were more dissatisfied with their bodies than heterosexual males (Williamson and Hartley 1998). Thus, if your son is homosexual, try to acknowledge the increased pressures to be thin in the gay male community. It will be helpful if he feels he can discuss these issues with you.

Special Considerations

In general, treatment plans for males and females with eating disorders are very similar. If you suspect your son has an eating disorder, we strongly recommend you get an evaluation. Eating disorders are often overlooked or misdiagnosed in males.

One of the best ways that you can help your male child is to help him handle the stigma associated with being male and having an eating disorder. Be careful not to contribute to this sense of shame. Males with eating disorders often feel isolated and lonely—even in treatment groups, where other clients are likely to be women. Some men with eating disorders struggle with the male gender stereotype, which unfairly demands, that men be more independent, competitive, physically strong, aggressive, and courageous than women (Kearney-Cooke and Steichen-Asch 1990). All the more reason your son needs your support.

Finally, there is some evidence to suggest that males with eating disorders have a higher rate of suicide attempts (Bramon-Bosch, Troop, and Treasure 2000). If you are concerned about this issue, consult a professional. Males have similar rates of recovery as females (Andersen 2002). You can best help your child by being supportive, optimistic, and patient during this time.

Ethnicity and Eating Disorders

Eating disorders have traditionally been considered a problem of white middle- and upper-class women and girls. Only recently have researchers and psychologists begun to acknowledge that eating disorders exist among men and women of color.

The current prevalence of eating disorders in the general population is estimated at between 1 and 3 percent (APA 1994). It is hard, however, to know if this is the prevalence across various ethnic groups. Some research suggests a lower prevalence of eating disorders among minority groups. Some psychologists feel that race may act as a protective factor against developing an eating disorder, particularly among

African-Americans. Other researchers feel that reports of lower rates of disordered eating in minorities may simply be the result of a white-centered treatment bias, or a lack of available services for people of color (Dolan 1991). Though we cannot be sure of the answer to this question, we do know that people of color can develop eating disorders and that the symptoms of eating problems among ethnic minorities look very similar to those of Caucasians (Le Grange, Telch, and Agras 1997).

Eating disorders can occur regardless of race, ethnicity, age, or sexual orientation. Researchers have hypothesized some risk factors specific to minority women. For example, minority women may experience racism, which leads to low self-worth and social isolation. This could lead to pressure to try to fit in with cultural beauty ideals (Crago, Shisslak, and Estes 1996).

African Americans

African-American women seem to have healthier attitudes than do Caucasian or Hispanic women when it comes to body image, food, and weight. African-American women seem to be more accepting of bodies of various sizes and builds and are less likely to be dissatisfied with their own bodies than are white women (Crago, Shisslak, and Estes 1996). African-American standards of beauty and weight may protect children and young adults from societal pressures to be thin and as a result may lower their risk for developing anorexia or bulimia nervosa (Rucker and Cash 1992).

Despite their more positive self-images and eating attitudes, African-American men and women can still develop eating disorders. There are magazine articles about dieting and advertisements for diet products directed at African-American consumers. While these articles may be in response to the fact that African-Americans are at higher risk for obesity, it is unclear how this trend will impact a generation of young boys and girls growing up under a newly developing weight consciousness.

Some research suggests that although African-American women may have a healthier self-image, they may also engage in unhealthy eating and weight-restricting behaviors. One study found that 71 percent of African-Americans stated that they had recently binged, 51 percent reported that they had recently dieted, 2 percent admitted to vomiting in order to purge the food they consumed, 5 percent acknowledged that they had used laxatives and 6 percent said they had used diuretics (Gray, Ford, and Kelly 1987). These findings suggest that a significant number of African-Americans have concerns about eating and weight.

Hispanics

Hispanics are the fastest growing population in the nation today, and the rates of eating disorders among Hispanics seem to be comparable to those of Caucasians. One study found that compared to African-Americans, Hispanics may be more likely to suffer from feelings of insecurity and inadequacy, which when coupled with feelings of social alienation may lead to eating problems (Rhea 1999).

Special Considerations

We still have much to learn about eating disorders in Hispanics and other ethnic minority groups such as Native Americans and Asians. Thankfully, the study of eating disorders among people of color is increasing as is awareness of eating disorders as a problem for people of all ethnic and socioeconomic backgrounds.

One important issue for every child and family is to find a therapist who feels like the right fit. Families who identify with racial or ethnic groups may want to take extra care to make sure that their therapist will understand the relevant cultural and societal issues. As a parent, try to talk to your child and understand how your child's view of his or her body is influenced by race and ethnicity. Be open to the possibility that racial or ethnic discrimination may have played a role in the development of the eating disorder. Your role as a parent will be to communicate with your child about these difficult issues and to help him or her feel supported and loved through the process of getting better.

Muscle Dysmorphic Disorder

In recent years, men have begun to experience pressure to build muscle, bulk up, and get larger in an effort to achieve an ideal male body type. A disorder, known as *muscle dysmorphia*, shares many of the same unhealthy behaviors, thoughts, and personality traits as the eating disorders. Individuals with muscle dysmorphia are preoccupied with becoming lean and muscular (Pope, et al. 1997). They exercise, lift weights, and regulate food in an extreme manner in an attempt to build muscle mass. Despite the fact that in most cases they are large and muscular already, people with muscle dysmorphia never feel big enough, and see their bodies as being smaller than they actually are (Pope, Phillips, and Olivardia 2000). This distorted body image, much like that seen in anorexia and bulimia, often leads to even more training, food restriction, and even bingeing and purging, all in an effort to "correct" bodies that are perceived as inadequate. Unfortunately, such a preoccupation with exercise and weight becomes an obsession and can begin to take over a person's life, often at the expense of developing careers, school, and relationships with friends, family, and loved ones.

Psychologically, people with muscle dysmorphia may suffer from a variety of co-occurring problems and may use their disorder to cope with other negative issues and events in their lives. Depression, anxiety, and obsessive compulsiveness can co-occur with muscle dysmorphia (Olivardia, Pope, and Hudson 2000). In addition to these problems, people suffering from this disorder often have low self-esteem, are insecure, and feel shame and embarrassment over their bodies (Pope, Phillips, and Olivardia 2000). This poor self-image leads to feeling uncomfortable in social settings, particularly in situations where they know their body is subject to evaluation by others and might be seen as too small (Yates 1999). Therefore, people with this disorder can become socially isolated, and avoid going out with friends or entering into relationships.

In addition to these difficult psychological issues, muscle dysmorphia can also have some dangerous physical consequences, such as causing strain and injury to muscles, joints, and bones (Pope, Phillips, and Olivardia 2000). Despite feeling physical pain, these individuals will rarely stop training or take time off for fear that they will lose weight and begin to get smaller.

There can be a dangerous risk for steroid use. Some body builders and athletes are willing to endure the harmful physical side effects of this drug in order to gain weight and muscle mass. One study found that up to 46 percent of male weight lifters with muscle dysmorphia reported using steroids, in comparison to only 7 percent of men without the disorder (Olivardia, Pope, and Hudson 2000). While all of the long-term side effects associated with steroid use are not clear, the known complications of this drug include changes in hormone levels, impotence, hypertension, steroid rage, heart attacks, and strokes (Yates 1999).

Special Considerations

Muscle dysmorphia is still in the process of being studied, so we have limited knowledge on its course and treatment. Many physicians may also not be familiar with this disorder, so if you are concerned your child may have it, you should see a doctor specializing in sports medicine, who may have a better idea of how your child's weight-lifting behaviors may be affecting his or her body.

Muscle dysmorphia is not just a physical disorder. If you suspect a problem, we recommend that you seek a therapist for your child. If possible, you will want to choose a professional who has had some experience with similar disorders. Preliminary studies have found cognitive behavioral therapy to be useful in addressing the problem behaviors of muscle dysmorphia and associated cognitive distortions about shape and weight (Pope, Phillips, and Olivardia 2000). Once in treatment, the therapist will work with your child to address some of the issues in his or her life that may be linked to the development and maintenance of these behaviors.

Specialized treatment for this disorder may be difficult to find, as it is a relatively new disorder. However, getting your son or daughter into treatment is essential for his or her health. You may need to be actively involved in finding an appropriate treatment for your child.

Athletes with Eating Disorders

Identifying eating disorders in athletes can be difficult. What is often considered abnormal in the general population (i.e. extreme views of shape and weight, excessive exercise, and severe dieting or fasting) is often seen in the athletic world as a mark of dedication and may even be encouraged by coaches. It is not known exactly how many athletes suffer from eating problems; estimates go as high as 25 percent (Byrne 2002). Many of the traits that can be found in athletes, including perfectionism, drive, competitiveness, and compulsiveness are also seen in people with eating disorders.

A recent review of the research on eating problems among female athletes found that those engaged in dance or performance sports (such as ballet, aerobics, cheerleadering) had higher rates of eating problems compared to girls who do not do this type of sport. Similarly "elite athletes" (professional athletes or those competing at a national or international level) were also at higher risk of eating problems than nonathletes. On the other hand, females who participate in non-elite sports that do not emphasize a lean body were at lower risk of eating problems than nonathletes. In other words, participating in most sports may actually protect your daughter from disordered eating. Playing a sport for fun and fitness may help build a sense of confidence that is not based upon appearance, and may help promote healthy eating and a healthy body image (Smolak, Murnen, and Ruble 2000).

Special Considerations

If your child is an athlete, your treatment team will need to include one more person: the coach. It is critical that all of the adults in your child's life be on the same page when it comes to health and safety. It is possible that your child's coach may be an important influence in getting your child into treatment. Contact your child's coach immediately to discuss your concerns.

If you find that you are at odds with you child's coach about your concerns, it is important to get some professional advice. Sometimes, due to the pressure of competition, coaches can lose perspective on the importance of health. Your child needs you to look out for his or her best interests, and it is not acceptable to place your child's health in jeopardy.

Finally, it will also be important for you and your child to work closely with a medical doctor and trainer during recovery. In particular, female athletes with eating disorders can experience something called the "female athlete triad," a syndrome that describes a pattern of disordered eating, loss of menstruation, and osteoporosis. If your child is an athlete and has an eating disorder, she may have an increased risk for bone density loss, so it will be important to have this assessed.

Paul's Story

Paul was overweight throughout his childhood. As a boy, he enjoyed large portions at meals and ate snack foods during the afternoons when he was home from school. Although his family was aware that he was overweight, they thought that his appetite was normal. He was encouraged to eat large amounts of food, and it was assumed that his body would know how much it needed for him to grow into a strong and healthy man.

When Paul was in high school, however, his weight became a bigger problem. Other boys started to tease him, and girls didn't seem interested in him. Paul felt like an outsider at his own school. During the summer before his sophomore year, he decided to change all of that. First, he stopped eating snacks, and then he reduced what he ate at meals. His weight started to drop. Next, he started to exercise, at first by walking, and eventually he was able to jog long distances. Paul felt better about himself, and others complimented him on the changes in his appearance.

By the time he returned to school for his sophomore year, Paul had lost twenty pounds and was physically fit. He joined a fitness club so that he would be able to continue exercising through the winter. There, he took fitness classes and used the treadmill, Stairmaster, and other equipment for cardiovascular workouts. As he continued to get in shape, girls took notice of him and other boys were friendlier toward him. Paul thought that these changes were great and that things would be even better if he lost more weight.

This was when Paul started to engage in unhealthy dieting behaviors and excessive exercising that would lead to an eating disorder. Paul started to skip meals and further restrict food at the meals he did eat. He also increased his workouts to a routine of at least two hours of exercise on most days. His weight dropped dramatically, and Paul felt tired, hungry, and dizzy at times. His family expressed their worry to him, but he assured them that he was fine. Paul was fearful that any attempts to change his routine would result in rapid weight gain and a return to being overweight.

Toward the end of his sophomore year, Paul was becoming more and more aware of feeling hungry. One Saturday afternoon, when the rest of his family was out of the house, he just couldn't take it anymore and headed for the kitchen in search of food. He ate pasta and cookies and cheese and ice cream. He felt excited to be eating after so many months of deprivation, but when the binge ended, he felt an enormous degree of guilt and anxiety. He decided that he needed to get rid of the food before it made him gain weight. Paul went into the bathroom and made himself vomit.

This cycle of bingeing and purging continued for several weeks when Paul's parents noticed that food seemed to be disappearing from the kitchen. Paul wanted to stop bingeing and purging, but he was afraid to talk with anyone about it. Then, one day his mother arrived home early when Paul was vomiting in the bathroom. She was extremely worried but decided that she would give her son some privacy and talk with him later.

When his mother spoke with him later that evening, Paul was embarrassed that she had heard him, appreciative that she didn't confront him right after he had purged, and ultimately relieved that he didn't have to be alone with this problem anymore. His mother suggested that he meet with a dietician to develop healthier eating habits, and she offered to go with him to this meeting if that would be helpful to him.

Paul decided to attend the first meeting on his own but agreed to have his mother attend a subsequent meeting so she could learn more about how to support him in making changes. Paul met with the dietician and learned a great deal about the importance of nutrition, and together they developed a plan to get Paul back on track with his eating. The dietician also recommended that he meet with a personal trainer to develop a more reasonable exercise plan, a physician for a physical exam, and a therapist for an eating disorder evaluation.

Jan's Story

Jan was a very bright fifteen-year-old who did well in school, had a lot of friends, and was active in her school's drama club and debate team. She got along well with others and seemed like a happy teenager to her teachers and friends. At home, however, Jan fought with her older brother, picked on her younger brothers, and argued with her parents. She usually seemed unhappy and angry, and this was frustrating to her parents, who always tried to please their children. Jan's parents were not only frustrated that their daughter was at times difficult at home, but they were also worried about her health. Jan was diabetic and would often argue with her parents about the management of her illness.

Jan's diabetes had been a source of conflict with her parents for many years. As a younger child, she had had to attend a lot of medical appointments, pay close attention to her diet, and comply with her insulin schedule. As she grew into a teenager, Jan's resentment about her illness intensified, and she became more argumentative at home.

By the time she was in high school, Jan realized that she could outsmart her body by adjusting her insulin amount if she wanted to eat a snack high in sugar. She also realized that she could use the insulin to lose weight. Sometimes, she wouldn't take her insulin with the hope of getting thinner. She thought that if she had to suffer with this illness, she could at least benefit from it by looking thin like the models in magazines and actresses on TV. She was proud of her discovery of this method of weight control until her doctor started to ask questions.

Jan's doctor noticed weight loss, incomplete food monitoring sheets, and irregular patterns in blood sugar levels. This was the first time these changes had happened, and her doctor was concerned. Knowing that insulin omission can be a form of purging and recognizing weight loss as a warning sign, the doctor spoke with Jan about the medical complications of using insulin in this way. Jan and the doctor also talked about Jan's family and her feelings about having diabetes. The doctor recommended that Jan and her parents consult with a therapist who specialized in eating disorders and was also knowledgeable about diabetes. Jan and her parents needed help identifying ways to talk about their frustrations calmly and to manage the diabetes without feeling overcontrolled or overcontrolling. Therapy was also recommended so that Jan could develop a healthier body image, especially in light of having a chronic illness.

Sam's Story

Sam had always been an athletic boy who loved to compete on sports teams. He grew up playing soccer, baseball, basketball, and hockey. While he excelled as an athlete, Sam was also a good-natured sportsman who enjoyed the camaraderie of playing as a member of a team. In high school, his talent for running was noticed by the cross-country coach, and Sam was asked to join that team. During the spring of his first year, Sam started his training as a long distance runner.

Sam was an outstanding cross-country runner, at first breaking records at his school and then breaking records across his state. The more races he won, the harder he trained. He thought about winning marathons and maybe even competing in the Olympics. Sam pushed himself so hard that his physical health was starting to be compromised. He burned more calories than he was consuming, but he didn't recognize how much weight he had lost, how pale he looked, or how isolated he had become. Sam was very focused on his goals and was losing sight of the importance of having a balanced life. He wanted to maintain a lean body but was starting to restrict himself to too few calories, and he was spending too many hours a day running. Sam needed help.

Sam's parents noticed that he was too focused on running to the exclusion of other activities and friendships, but Sam got angry whenever they brought this up with him. His coach talked with him about training less and paying closer attention to nutrition, but Sam assured him that he was doing fine and feeling healthy. Even his friends talked with him about how he spent all of his time running and rarely saw them anymore, but Sam thought that they were just jealous about his accomplishments. Finally, Sam's parents decided that Sam's health was at risk and he needed to see a physician. His coach and parents told him that he had to have a medical evaluation before he could continue participating on the team.

Sam's doctor was very concerned about Sam's low weight and inadequate nutrition, especially in the context of cross-country training for many hours a day. And, when Sam's vital signs were unstable during the physical exam, the doctor insisted that he stop running until his nutrition improved, his weight increased, and his vital signs stabilized.

Sam was also referred to a psychologist for additional support and guidance with these changes, but didn't want to see a therapist. Meanwhile, his parents and coach agreed with the doctor's decisions and recommendations. Sam would not be allowed to run cross-country until his doctor approved it. Sam's parents were relieved that their son was getting the medical attention he needed, and they planned to do some research on eating disorders among boys and athletes. They wanted to read more about this in order to develop ways to support their son and talk with him about the value of meeting with a therapist.

Creating Solutions

After reading this chapter, you may have found some information that relates to your child's situation. Take a few moments to make a list of what you feel is unique about your child's situation and think about how you might solve problems differently.

Here are some questions to consider:

Are there ways in which your child seems to fit the "typical" profile of someone with an eating disorder? _____

_____

_____

Are there other ways in which he or she does not fit? _____

_____

_____

_____

What are some unique characteristics of your child's experience that need to be addressed in treatment? _____

_____

_____

_____

Are there other significant people (such as coaches or other medical professionals) who should be involved in treatment? _____

_____

_____

It is entirely understandable if you are feeling overwhelmed about how to help your child deal with his or her eating disorder and other unique challenges. Try to take a deep breath. We hope it is clear from reading this chapter that it is not unusual for someone with an eating disorder to also have another challenge, such as another psychological or medical problem. This means that many professionals are familiar with and know how to manage these different concerns, so talk to someone who can give you the tools you need to best facilitate your child's recovery.

A Final Word

We hope this book has given you a sense of hope and started your family down the path to recovery. While it is true that eating disorders are serious mental health problems with severe psychological and physical consequences, it is also true that recovery and health are possible.

Many people imagine that once a person has a mental illness, it means they will always have it and can never lead a "normal," healthy life. The good news is that this is simply not true, and the potential payoffs from treatment are well worth the investment. Research demonstrates that for the large majority of people, treatment is effective and can have long-lasting results. This means that your child has good odds of not only getting well, but also staying well.

As you and your family work toward recovery, remember that you are not alone. Sadly, eating disorders are a common problem. Although people who struggle with eating disorders and their families often feel alone and misunderstood, remember that many people have these problems. The desire to be thin and restrict food intake, which are common early signs of an eating disorder, are unfortunately a hallmark of Western society. While people understand the motivation behind eating disorders, they do not understand the seriousness of the problem and how easily extreme dieting can catch a vulnerable person in a dangerous cycle of disordered eating and low self-esteem.

You can help raise understanding of both the seriousness of eating disorders and the ways that society contributes to their development. Remember that although food is critically involved in the symptoms of eating disorders, the disorders themselves are real mental health problems. As the disorder worsens, a person's functioning at work or school, and in their relationships, as well as their happiness, can become severely impaired. This means that you should not shy away from seeking professional help if you are concerned that your child may be suffering. The earlier your child gets treatment, the better his or her chances for a full and lasting recovery.

There is a lot you can do at home, and perhaps in family therapy, to help this recovery. You can provide an example of healthy eating and exercise and demonstrate love for your children as people, independent of their appearance or weight. Keep in mind that criticizing your children's shape or weight can have a negative impact on the way that your children view themselves and their bodies and may set the stage for an eating disorder. Even though comments about shape and weight may seem harmless or even helpful, they can negatively influence a child who may already be susceptible to developing an eating disorder. Parents' own insecurities about food and weight can transfer to their children, so work together as a family to appreciate your bodies and your health.

Above all, do not give up hope and do not blame yourself. Blaming yourself does not help anyone, and you cannot fix this problem alone. Remember that there are many possible factors that contribute to the development of an eating disorder. For any one person, the reasons behind the illness are complex. Not only is it inaccurate and unfair to hold yourself entirely responsible for your child's behavior, but it also does not help your child get better.

Instead, focus on the present and the future. Think about how family and friends can work together to promote everyone's health, including your own. You will likely choose to make changes in your home to help your child recover more easily, but this does not mean that you and your family were the reason your child became sick. It is your job as a parent to love and support your child and to help find the resources your child needs. We recommend that you to work together during this difficult time, and we wish your family the best of luck and good health.

Eating Attitudes Test (EAT-26)

The EAT-26 (Garner, et al. 1982) is one of the most popular (and best-researched) questionnaires for evaluating characteristics of eating disorders. So, even though it cannot give you a diagnosis for your child (you will need to see a professional to determine that), this measure can help you learn a lot about the symptoms of eating disorders.

By filling out the questionnaire, your child can learn more about eating problems and identify his or her own specific concerns. Try to be as supportive as possible and keep in mind that acknowledging these problems can be extremely scary. Your child may feel frightened about recognizing the problems, especially in writing, and embarrassed about sharing the results with you. It may be that your child would prefer to fill out the questionnaire privately and not share the answers with you. Although this is understandably difficult for you as a concerned parent, we suggest that you respect this wish.

If your child is willing to complete the survey, encourage him or her to fill it out in a quiet place without distractions. The survey takes about ten minutes to complete. Whether your child chooses to complete the survey alone or with you there, make yourself available to talk about it. Ideally, you both want to gain understanding about what things are working well and what areas are more difficult.

Please check a response for each of the following questions:

	Always	Usually	Often	Sometimes	Rarely	Never
1. Am terrified about being overweight.	☐	☐	☐	☐	☐	☐
2. Avoid eating when I am hungry.	☐	☐	☐	☐	☐	☐
3. Find myself preoccupied with food.	☐	☐	☐	☐	☐	☐
4. Have gone on eating binges where I feel that I may not be able to stop.	☐	☐	☐	☐	☐	☐
5. Cut my food into small pieces.	☐	☐	☐	☐	☐	☐
6. Aware of the calorie content of foods that I eat.	☐	☐	☐	☐	☐	☐
7. Particularly avoid food with a high carbohydrate content (i.e., bread, rice, potatoes, etc.).	☐	☐	☐	☐	☐	☐
8. Feel that others would prefer if I ate more.	☐	☐	☐	☐	☐	☐
9. Vomit after I have eaten.	☐	☐	☐	☐	☐	☐
10. Feel extremely guilty after eating.	☐	☐	☐	☐	☐	☐
11. Am preoccupied with a desire to be thinner.	☐	☐	☐	☐	☐	☐
12. Think about burning up calories when I exercise.	☐	☐	☐	☐	☐	☐
13. Other people think that I am too thin.	☐	☐	☐	☐	☐	☐
14. Am preoccupied with the thought of having fat on my body.	☐	☐	☐	☐	☐	☐
15. Take longer than others to eat my meals.	☐	☐	☐	☐	☐	☐
16. Avoid foods with sugar in them.	☐	☐	☐	☐	☐	☐
17. Eat diet foods.	☐	☐	☐	☐	☐	☐
18. Feel that food controls my life.	☐	☐	☐	☐	☐	☐
19. Display self-control around food.	☐	☐	☐	☐	☐	☐

20. Feel that others pressure me to eat. □ □ □ □ □ □

21. Give too much time and thought to food. □ □ □ □ □ □

22. Feel uncomfortable after eating sweets. □ □ □ □ □ □

23. Engage in dieting behavior. □ □ □ □ □ □

24. Like my stomach to be empty. □ □ □ □ □ □

25. Enjoy trying new rich foods. □ □ □ □ □ □

26. Have the impulse to vomit after meals. □ □ □ □ □ □

Scoring the Eating Attitudes Test

To score the EAT-26, you only have to count the items marked "always," "usually," or "often." This is because the other responses ("sometimes," "rarely," and "never") are less severe ratings. For each item marked "always," assign 3 points. For each item marked "usually," assign 2 points. For each item marked "often," assign 1 point. Now add up the item scores to determine the total score. The only exception to this rule is item 25, which has been shaded in gray. This item is worded in such a way that a high score on this item would indicate a non-disordered response. So, item 25 should be scored in the following way: "never" equals 3 points; "rarely" equals 2 points; "sometimes" equals 1 point. Simply add this item's score to the total, and you are all done.

Comparing Scores

When this questionnaire is used to screen for eating disorders, a cutoff of 20 is usually used as the marker to indicate the need for further evaluation because the symptoms may be indicative of disordered eating. Thus, for those who score 20 or above, we recommend a professional evaluation. Keep in mind that this cutoff should not be followed in a rigid way; for example, for someone who scores 18 and shows many of the warning signs discussed in chapter 1, we still recommend a professional consultation. Another way to think about an EAT score is to compare it to the average score for people in different groups. Researchers have found that women with eating disorders score 36.1 on average on the EAT-26, whereas women without an eating disorder score 9.9 on average (Garner, et al. 1982). You can think of these numbers as "norms" for the groups and use them as a point of comparison.

Appendix B

Sample Daily Food Record

Time	Food and Amount	Location

We Want to Hear from You!

There is still a lot we do not know about how best to advise parents on the role they can play in helping their child recover from an eating disorder. Therefore, we view this guide as a work in progress and recognize that you are the real experts on what is best for your family! That is why we need your help to revise this resource based on the feedback we get from you. Your answers can be used to help others, so after reading the book, please take a moment to complete this short questionnaire, and let us know how we are doing so far. . . .

Please circle the number (from 1–5) that best reflects your answer to the following questions . . .

	Very Poor	Poor	Average	Good	Very Good
1. Overall, how useful was this guide?	1	2	3	4	5
2. How would you rate this guide compared to other resources you have used?	1	2	3	4	5
3. How effectively did this guide cover the issues that are important to you?	1	2	3	4	5
4. When you tried to implement the suggestions from this guide, how satisfied were you with the outcomes?	1	2	3	4	5
5. To what extent has this guide positively influenced communication patterns within your family?	1	2	3	4	5

6. What aspects of this guide did you find most helpful?

_____

_____

_____

_____

_____

7. Which suggestions did you try, and how did they work with your family?

_____

_____

_____

_____

8. What other questions do you have that this guide has not addressed?

_____

_____

_____

_____

9. What other advice would you want to offer to parents?

_____

_____

_____

_____

10. What other resources (books, Web sites, organizations, etc.) would you recommend adding to our list?

_____

_____

_____

_____

Thank you for your help

The completed questionnaire can be mailed to:

Yale Center for Eating and Weight Disorders
Yale University Department of Psychology
P. O. Box 208205
New Haven, CT 06520-8205

Resources

This resource list is designed to help you gather more information on those topics that are of particular interest to you and your family. We have included a list of helpful organizations and their Web sites, grouped under the following resource headings: general mental health, eating disorders, healthy eating, parenting, finding an eating disorder therapist, and eating disorder publications.

In addition, we have recommended further reading on the following topics: general information for families and friends; general information for children and adolescents; what to expect in therapy; understanding the causes of eating disorders; parenting resources; healthy eating resources; and information on special populations.

Helpful Organizations and Their Web Sites

General Mental Health

National Mental Health Association (NMHA)
Phone: (800) 969-6642; Stigma Watch Line (800) 969-NMHA;
TTY line (800) 433-5959
Web site: http://www.nmha.org/

National Institute of Mental Health (NIMH; Public Inquiries and Information Resources)
Phone: (301) 443-4513
Web site: http://www.nimh.nih.gov/

American Psychological Association (APA)
Phone: (800) 964-2000 (Give an operator your zip code, and he or she will help you locate and connect with your local referral system.)
Web site: http://www.apa.org

Eating Disorders

National Eating Disorder Referral and Information Center
Phone: (858) 792-7463
Web site: http://www.edreferral.com

National Eating Disorders Association
Phone: (206) 382-3587
Web site: http://www.nationaleatingdisorders.org

Anorexia Nervosa and Related Eating Disorders
Phone: (503) 344-1144
Web site: http://www.anred.com

Harvard Eating Disorders Center
Phone: (888) 236-1188, ext. 100
Web site: http://www.hedc.org

National Association of Anorexia Nervosa and Associated Disorders
Phone: (847) 831-3438
Web site: http://www.anad.org

The Something Fishy Web Site on Eating Disorders
Web site: http://www.something-fishy.org

Healthy Eating

American Dietetic Association's Nationwide Nutrition Network
Phone: (800) 366-1655 (National Center for Nutrition and Dietetics's consumer nutrition information line)
Web site: http://www.eatright.org

HealthAtoZ.com
Web site: http://www.healthatoz.com/atoz/lifestyles/food/hfoodindex.html

Health World On-line
Web site: http://www.healthy.net

Parenting

Parenting Today's Teen
Phone: (360) 753-2965
Web site: http://www.parentingteens.com

Finding an Eating Disorder Therapist

Eating Disorder Referral and Information Center
Phone: (858) 792-7463
Web site: www.edreferral.com

4therapy.com network
Phone: (888) 4therapy
Web site: www.4therapy.com

Eating Disorder Publications

Gurze Books
Phone: (800) 756-7533
Web site: www.gurze.net

Suggested Reading

General Information for Families and Friends

Anorexia Nervosa: A Survival Guide for Families, Friends and Sufferers, by J. Treasure, Psychology Press, 1997. A book written for people suffering from an eating disorder and their families. Provides comprehensive and easy-to-read information on the causes and consequences of anorexia nervosa. Addresses how to discuss the problem with your loved one and how to access treatment.

Eating Disorder Sourcebook: A Comprehensive Guide to the Causes, Treatment and Prevention of Eating Disorders, by C. Costin, Gurze Books, 1999. Written for people suffering from eating disorders, their loved ones, and the professionals who work closely with them, this book explores what eating disorders are and where they come from and addresses the psychological, medical, and nutritional issues that underlie them. Provides proactive advice on how to deal with an eating disorder on a day-to-day basis.

Bulimia: A Guide for Friends and Family (Psychology Series), by R. T. Sherman and R. A. Thompson, Jossey-Bass Publishers, 1997. An accessible introduction to bulimia nervosa. This book provides a good foundation for coming to understand the behaviors, thoughts, and emotions behind this disorder. The question and answer sections address many of parents' most pressing concerns.

Surviving an Eating Disorder: Strategies for Families and Friends, by M. Siegel, J. Brisman, and M. Weinshel, HarperCollins Publishers, 1997. A clearly written resource guide that provides a number of practical strategies for friends and families dealing with anorexia nervosa, bulimia nervosa, or binge eating disorder. It is based upon the latest scientific knowledge and the clinical experiences of the authors, who are specialists in the field.

General Information for Children and Adolescents

Bulimia Nervosa: The Secret Cycle of Bingeing and Purging (Teen Health Library of Eating Disorder Prevention), by L. Burby, Gurze Books, 1998, and *Anorexia Nervosa: When Food Is the Enemy (Teen Health Library of Eating Disorder Prevention),* by E. Smith, Gurze Books, 1998. These two books, part of the Teen Health Library of Eating Disorder Prevention series, are written in an easy-to-read, interactive style that is accessible to any teen or young adult, ages eleven and up. These books provide a general overview of the major eating disorders and focus in on the specifics of anorexia and bulimia nervosa, providing a detailed description of the causes and consequences of these disorders. Ideas presented within the books help adolescents to cope with and/or prevent eating problems.

What to Expect in Therapy

The Essential Guide to Mental Health: The Most Comprehensive Guide to the New Psychiatry for Popular Family Use, by J. M. Gorman, St. Martin's Press, 1998. This book takes you step by step through the therapy process and provides insight on everything from choosing a therapist to attending a first session and understanding a diagnosis. This resource will help you to navigate the major forms of treatment and to decide what you should expect from each. A useful guide for anyone seeking professional psychiatric help for mental illness.

Columbia University College of Physicians and Surgeons: Complete Home Guide to Mental Health, by F.I. Kass, J.M. Oldham, H. Pardes, and L.B. Morris, Henry Holt and Company, 1992. An accessible guide to understanding mental illness in the family. Helps the reader to decide when to seek treatment, how to find a therapist, what to expect in the first session, and much more.

The Essential Guide to Psychiatric Drugs, by J. M. Gorman, St. Martin's Press, 1998. A detailed yet easy-to-understand guide to psychiatric medications, useful for anyone who is considering or who is using medication for mental illness. Provides information on the dosage, cost, benefits, and potential side effects of most major psychiatric drugs. A useful tool for those who are interested in learning more about medication and the treatment of mental illness.

Understanding the Causes of Eating Disorders

Reviving Ophelia: Saving the Souls of Adolescent Girls, by M. Pipher, Ballantine Books, 1995. This book provides an insightful examination of America's adolescent girls. Dr. Pipher explores the factors that push so many young females to extremes of depression, suicide, eating disorders, and addiction. This book examines the pressures that our media and society place on young females as they transition to adulthood.

Body Wars: Making Peace with Women's Bodies, by M. Maine, Gurze Books, 1999. Examines the societal factors that cause women to become vulnerable to eating disorders. Contains strategies for teaching your daughter how to confront false messages of dieting and the thin body ideal promoted by print and television media.

Parenting Resources

Positive Discipline for Teenagers: Empowering Your Teen and Yourself through Kind and Firm Parenting, by J. Nelsen and L. Lott, Prima Publishing, 2000. Teenagers of the twenty-first century face unique challenges. Using a workbook format, this resource helps you to identify areas where your relationship with your child may need work, and to formulate a plan for dealing with difficult or frustrating issues. Chapters devoted to parent-teen conflict and communication provide good advice for both parents and their children.

Get Out of My Life, but First Could You Drive Me and Cheryl to the Mall? A Parent's Guide to the New Teenager, by A. E. Wolf, HarperCollins, 1991. This humorously written book reframes difficult teenage behaviors as examples of the teenager's effort to become independent from his or her parents. The examples in the book provide an opportunity to distinguish "normal" teenage rebellion from more serious behavioral problems.

Your Adolescent: Emotional, Behavioral, Cognitive Development from Early Adolescence Through the Teen Years, by the American Academy of Child and Adolescent Psychiatry, HarperCollins, 1999. This book presents a comprehensive and user-friendly look at adolescence, its stages and its issues. The authors explore the physical, psychological, and social changes that occur at each stage of adolescence. The book addresses important general issues such as dating, friends, and school, and matters of more serious concern, including drug and alcohol abuse, sex, mental health issues, and chronic illness. Later chapters help you distinguish between normal and abnormal behavior.

Parent Effectiveness Training: The Proven Program for Raising Responsible Children, by T. Gordon, Three Rivers Press, 2000. A guide for teaching parents how to communicate with their children more effectively. Dr. Gordon's techniques help parents to become both better listeners and communicators so that they can teach their children how to express their own feelings and needs successfully. Explores a number of important topics including parent roles and styles, parent-child conflicts, parental authority and permissiveness, and strategies of effective parent-child communication.

Healthy Eating Resources

The American Dietetic Association's Complete Food and Nutrition Guide, by R. Larson-Duyff, Chronimed Publishing, 1996. An easy-to-read guide to nutrition and exercise for the entire family. Combines the latest research on food and physical activity with practical tips on how to eat well and increase fitness.

Secrets of Feeding a Healthy Family, by E. Satter, Kelcy Press, 1999. A great resource for helping you and your family understand what good nutrition means. Contains recipes and hints for food shopping and preparation.

Total Nutrition: The Only Guide You'll Ever Need, by V. Herbert, G.J. Subak-Sharpe, and T. Stopler-Kasdan, St. Martin's Press, 1995. A complete guide to nutrition and healthy eating, this book helps the reader to understand nutrition across the life span, providing information on everything from fat and cholesterol, to proteins and sugars, vitamins and supplements.

Special Populations

The Adonis Complex: How to Identify, Treat and Prevent Body Obsession in Men and Boys, by H.G. Pope, K.A. Phillips, and R. Olivardia, Touchstone Books, 2002. A clearly written resource for men who struggle with eating and body image disorders. Discusses a variety of shape and weight issues that affect boys and men of all ages, and explores the experiences of men who suffer from problems such as anorexia nervosa, binge eating disorder, steroid use, and an extreme obsession with exercise and muscles. Additional information for the loved ones and friends of men who struggle with these problems is provided.

The Athletic Woman's Survival Guide: How to Win the Battle Against Eating Disorders, Amenorrhea and Osteoporosis, by C. Otis and R. Goldingay, Gurze Books, 2000. Explores the eating, training, and performance pressures on female athletes today. Gives practical insight on nutrition and energy intake, how to deal with physical injury, and how to communicate with your child's coach once you learn that there is a problem. Empowers the reader with relevant information that can be used by friends, families, coaches, communities, and the athlete herself to avoid eating and exercise disorders and to help maintain peak performance in a safe and healthy way.

References

American Psychiatric Association. 1994. *Diagnostic and Statistical Manual of Mental Disorders IV*. Washington, D.C.: American Psychiatric Publishing.

Andersen, A.E. 1999. Males with eating disorders. In *Eating Disorders: A Guide to Medical Care and Complications*, edited by P.S. Mehler and A.E. Andersen. Baltimore: Johns Hopkins University Press.

———. 2002. Eating disorders in males. In *Eating Disorders and Obesity: A Comprehensive Handbook*. 2nd ed., edited by C.G Fairburn and K.D. Brownell. London: The Guilford Press.

Andersen, A.E., and L. DiDomenico. 1992. Diet vs. shape content of popular male and female magazines: A dose response relationship to the incidence of eating disorders? *International Journal of Eating Disorders* 11(3):283–287.

Apple, R.F. 1999. Interpersonal therapy for bulimia nervosa. *Journal of Clinical Psychology/ In Session: Psychotherapy in Practice* 55(6):715–725.

Baran, S.A., T.E. Weltzon, and W.H. Kaye. 1995. Low discharge weight and outcome in anorexia nervosa. *American Journal of Psychiatry* 152:1070–1072.

Baumrind, D. 1991. The influence of parenting styles on adolescent competence and substance use. *Journal of Early Adolescence* 11:56–95.

Beaumont, P.J. 2002. Clinical presentation of anorexia nervosa and bulimia nervosa. In *Eating Disorders and Obesity: A Comprehensive Handbook*, edited by C.G. Fairburn and K.D. Brownell. New York: The Guilford Press.

Beren, S.E., H.A. Hayden, D.E. Wilfley, and C.M. Grilo. 1996. The influence of sexual orientation on body dissatisfaction in adult men and women. *International Journal of Eating Disorders* 20(2):135–141.

Blair, S.N., and S. Brodney. 1999. The effects of physical inactivity and obesity on morbidity and mortality: Current evidence and research issues. *Medicine and Science in Sports Exercise* 31(Suppl): 646–662.

Bordo, S. 1993. *Unbearable Weight: Feminism, Western Culture and the Body.* Berkeley: University of California Press.

Bramon-Bosch, E., N.A. Troop, and J.L. Treasure. 2000. Eating disorders in males: A comparison with female patients. *European Eating Disorders Review* 8:321–328.

Braun, D.L., S.R. Sunday, and K.A. Halmi. 1994. Psychiatric comorbidity in patients with eating disorders. *Psychological Medicine* 24:859–867.

Brownell, K.D. 1991. Dieting and the search for the perfect body: Where physiology and culture collide. *Behavior Therapy* 22(1):1–12.

Brownell, K.D., G.A. Marlatt, E. Lichtenstein, and G.T. Wilson. 1986. Understanding and preventing relapse. *American Psychologist* 41(7):765–782.

Bryant-Waugh, R., and B. Lask. 2002. Childhood-onset eating disorders. In *Eating Disorders and Obesity: A Comprehensive Handbook*, edited by C.G. Fairburn and K.D. Brownell. New York: The Guilford Press.

Bulik, C. 2002. Anxiety, depression, and eating disorders. In *Eating Disorders and Obesity: A Comprehensive Handbook*, edited by C.G. Fairburn and K.D. Brownell. New York: The Guilford Press.

Byrne, S.M. 2002. Sport, occupation and eating disorders. In *Eating Disorders and Obesity: A Comprehensive Handbook. 2nd ed.,* edited by C.G Fairburn and K.D. Brownell. London: The Guilford Press.

Cash, T.F. 1997. *The Body Image Workbook.* New York: MJF Books.

Chen, E. In press. A comparison of group and individual cognitive behavioral treatments for patients with bulimia nervosa. *International Journal of Eating Disorders.*

Collins, M.E. 1991. Body figure perceptions and preferences among preadolescent children. *International Journal of Eating Disorders* 10(1):1–13.

Crago, M., C.M. Shisslak, and L.S. Estes. 1996. Eating disturbances among American minority groups. *International Journal of Eating Disorders* 19(3):239–248.

Crisp, A.H., J.S. Callender, C. Halek, and G.L. Hsu. 1992. Long-term mortality in anorexia nervosa: A twenty-year follow-up of the St.

George's and Aberdeen cohorts. *British Journal of Psychiatry* 161:104–107.

Dare, C., and I. Eisler. 2002. Family therapy and eating disorders. In *Eating Disorders and Obesity: A Comprehensive Handbook*, edited by C.G. Fairburn and K.D. Brownell. New York: The Guilford Press.

Dare, C., I. Eisler, M. Colahan, C. Crowther, R. Senior, and E. Asen. 1995. Listening heart and the chi-square: Clinical and empirical perceptions in the family therapy of anorexia nervosa. *Journal of Family Therapy* 17:31–57.

De Zwaan, M., J.E. Mitchell, H.C. Seim, S.M. Specker, R. L. Pyle, N.C. Raymond, and R. B. Crosby. 1994. Eating related and general psychopathology in obese females with binge eating disorder. *International Journal of Eating Disorders* 15(1):43–52.

Devlin, M.J. 2002. Pharmacological treatment of binge eating disorder. In *Eating Disorders and Obesity: A Comprehensive Handbook*, edited by C.G. Fairburn and K.D. Brownell. New York: The Guilford Press.

Dolan, B. 1991. Cross-cultural aspects of anorexia nervosa and bulimia: A review. *International Journal of Eating Disorders* 10(1):67–79.

Drewnowski, A., and D.K. Yee. 1987. Men and body image: Are males satisfied with their body weight? *Psychosomatic Medicine* 49(6): 626–634.

Drewnowski, A., D.K. Yee, and D.D. Krahn. 1988. Bulimia in college women: Incidence and recovery rates. *American Journal of Psychiatry* 145:753–755.

Eisen, S.V., B. Clarridge, V. Stringfellow, J.A. Shaul, and P.D. Cleary. 2001. In *Improving Mental Health Care: Commitment to Quality*, edited by B. Dickey and L.I. Sederer. Washington, D.C.: Psychiatric Publishing, Inc.

Eisler, I. 1995. Family models of eating disorders. In *Handbook of Eating Disorders: Theory, Treatment and Research*, edited by G.I. Szmukler, C. Dare, and J. Treasure. Chichester, England: John Wiley and Sons.

Fahy, T.A., and G.F. Russell. 1993. Outcome and prognostic variables in bulimia nervosa. *International Journal of Eating Disorders* 14(2):135–145.

Fairburn, C.G. 1997. Interpersonal psychotherapy for bulimia nervosa. In *Handbook of Treatment for Eating Disorders. Vol. 2*, edited by D.M. Garner, and P.E. Garfinkel. New York: The Guilford Press.

Fairburn, C.G., M.D. Marcus, and G.T. Wilson. 1993. Cognitive behavioral treatment for binge eating and bulimia nervosa: A comprehensive treatment manual. In *Binge Eating: Nature, Assessment and*

Treatment, edited by C.G. Fairburn and G.T. Wilson. New York: The Guilford Press.

Fallon, P., and S.A. Wonderlich. 1997. Sexual abuse and other forms of trauma. In *Handbook of Treatment for Eating Disorders. Vol. 2*, edited by D.M. Garner and P.E. Garfinkel. New York: Guilford Press.

Fichter, M.M., and N. Quadflieg. 1999. Six-year course and outcome of anorexia nervosa. *International Journal of Eating Disorders* 26(4):359–385.

Garfinkel, P.E., and B.T. Walsh. 1997. Drug therapies. In *Handbook of Treatment for Eating Disorders. Vol. 2*, edited by D.M. Garner and P.E. Garfinkel. New York: The Guilford Press.

Garner, D.M., and L.D. Needleman. 1997. Sequencing and integration of treatments. In *Handbook of Treatments for Eating Disorders. Vol. 2*, edited by D.M. Garner and P.E. Garfinkel. New York: The Guilford Press.

Garner, D.M., M.P. Olmsted, Y. Bohr, and P.E. Garfinkel. 1982. The Eating Attitudes Test: Psychometric features and clinical correlates. *Psychological Medicine* 12(4):871–878.

Garner, D.M., W. Rockert, R. Davis, M.V. Garner, M.P. Olmstead, and M. Eagle. 1993. Comparison of cognitive-behavioral and supportive-expressive therapy for bulimia nervosa. *American Journal of Psychiatry* 150:37–46.

Garner, D.M., K.M. Vitousek, and K.M. Pike. 1997. Reasoning error categories among eating disordered people. In *Handbook of Treatment for Eating Disorders. 2nd ed.*, edited by D.M. Garner, and P.E. Garfinkel. New York: The Guilford Press.

Gleaves, D.H., K.P. Eberenz, and M.C. May. 1998. Scope and significance of posttraumatic symptomatology among women hospitalized for an eating disorder. *International Journal of Eating Disorders* 24(2):147–156.

Gray, J.J., K. Ford, and L.M. Kelly. 1987. The prevalence of bulimia in a black college population. *International Journal of Eating Disorders* 6:733–740.

Grilo, C.M. 2002. Binge eating disorder. In *Eating Disorders and Obesity: A Comprehensive Handbook. 2nd ed.*, edited by C.G Fairburn and K.D. Brownell. London: The Guilford Press.

Heatherton, T.F., and R.F. Baumeister. 1991. Binge eating as an escape from self-awareness. *Psychological Bulletin* 110(1):86–108.

Hill, A.J. 2002. Prevalence and demographics of dieting. In *Eating Disorders and Obesity: A Comprehensive Handbook. 2nd ed.*, edited by C.G Fairburn and K.D. Brownell. London: The Guilford Press.

Holderness, C.C., J. Brooks-Gunn, and M.P. Warren. 1994. Co-morbidity of eating disorders and substance abuse review of the literature. *International Journal of Eating Disorders* 16(1):1–34.

Hsu, L.G. 1989. The gender gap in eating disorders: Why are the eating disorders more common among women? *Clinical Psychology Review* 9(3):393–407.

International Food and Information Council Foundation. 1998. *Review, Sorting Out Facts about Fat*. Retrieved from the World Wide Web: www.ific.org

International Food Information Council Foundation. 2000. *Fad Diets—Look Before You Leap*. Retrieved from the World Wide Web: www.ific.org

Johnson, B.M., S. Shulman, and W.A. Collins. 1991. Systematic patterns of parenting as reported by adolescents: Developmental differences and implications for psychosocial outcomes. *Journal of Adolescent Research* 6:235–252.

Kearney-Cooke, A., and P. Steichen-Asch. 1990. Men, body image and eating disorders. In *Males with Eating Disorders*, edited by A.E. Andersen. New York: Brunner/Mazel Publishers.

Keel, P.K., and J.E. Mitchell. 1997. Outcome in bulimia nervosa. *American Journal of Psychiatry* 154(3):313–321.

Keys, A., J., A. Brozek, and A. Henschel. 1950. *The Biology of Human Starvation. Vols 1–2*. Minneapolis: University of Minnesota Press.

Laessle, R.G., P.J.V. Beumont, P. Butow, W. Lennerts, M. O'Connor, K. Pirke, and S. Touyz. 1991. A comparison of nutritional management and stress management in the treatment of bulimia nervosa. *British Journal of Psychiatry* 159:250–261.

Lask, B., and R. Bryant-Waugh. 1997. Prepubertal eating disorders. In *Handbook of Treatment for Eating Disorders. Vol. 2*, edited by D.M. Garner and P.E. Garfinkel. New York: The Guilford Press.

Lazarus, R.S., and S. Folkman. 1984. *Stress, Appraisal and Coping*. New York: Springer.

Le Grange, D., C.F. Telch, and W.S. Agras. 1997. Eating and general psychopathology in a sample of Caucasian and ethnic minority subjects. *International Journal of Eating Disorders* 21:285–293.

Lester, R., and T. Petrie. 1995. Personality and physical correlates of bulimic symptomatology among Mexican-American female college students. *Journal of Counseling Psychology* 42:199–203.

———. 1998. Physical, psychological, and societal correlates of bulimic symptomatology among African American college women. *Journal of Counseling Psychology* 45:315–321.

Levine, M.P., and L. Hill. 1991. *How to Help a Friend: The IMAD Approach.* National Eating Disorders Association. Retrieved from the World Wide Web: www.nationaleatingdisorders.org.

Lock, J., D. Le Grange, W.S. Argas, and C. Dare. 2001. *Treatment Manual for Anorexia Nervosa: A Family-Based Approach.* New York: The Guilford Press.

Maine, M. 2001. *Tips for Becoming a Critical Viewer of the Media.* National Eating Disorders Association. Retrieved from the World Wide Web: www.nationaleatingdisorders.org.

Marcus, M.D. 1997. Adapting treatment for patients with binge-eating disorder. In *Handbook of Treatment for Eating Disorders. 2nd ed.*, edited by D.M. Garner and P.E. Garfinkel. New York: The Guilford Press.

Marcus, M.D., R.R. Wing, L. Ewing, E. Kern, W. Gooding, and M. McDermott. 1990. Psychiatric disorders among obese binge eaters. *International Journal of Eating Disorders* 9(1):69–77.

Miller, W.R., and S. Rollnick. 1991. *Motivational Interviewing: Preparing People to Change Addictive Behavior.* New York: The Guilford Press.

National Eating Disorders Association (NEDA). 2001. www.nationaleatingdisorders.org.

Nichter, M. 2000. *Fat Talk: What Girls and Their Parents Say about Dieting.* Cambridge: Harvard University Press.

O'Connor, M., S. Touyz, and P. Beumont. 1988. Nutritional management and dietary counseling in bulimia nervosa: Some preliminary observations. *International Journal of Eating Disorders* 7(5):657–662.

Olivardia, R., H.G. Pope, and J.I. Hudson. 2000. Muscle dysmorphia in male weight-lifters: A case-control study. *American Journal of Psychiatry* 157:1291–1296.

Pennebaker, J.W. 1989. Confession, inhibition, and disease. In *Advances in Experimental Social Psychology*, edited by L. Berkowitz. New York: Academic Press.

Pennebaker, J.W., J.K. Kiecolt-Glaser, and R. Glaser. 1988. Disclosure of traumas and immune function: Health implications for psychotherapy. *Journal of Consulting Clinical Psychology* 56:239–245.

Peterson, C.B., and J.E. Mitchell. 1999. Psychosocial and pharmacological treatment of eating disorders: A review of research findings. *Journal of Clinical Psychology* 55(6):685–697.

Pike, K.M., and J. Rodin. 1991. Mothers, daughters and disordered eating. *Journal of Abnormal Psychology* 100(2):198–204.

Pope, H.G., A.J. Gruber, P. Choi, P. Olivardia, and K.A. Phillips. 1997. Muscle dysmorphia: An underrecognized form of body dysmorphic disorder. *Psychosomatics* 38(6):548–557.

Pollice, C., W.H. Kaye, C.G. Greeno, and T.E. Weltzin. 1997. Relationship of depression, anxiety, and obsessionality to state of illness in anorexia nervosa. *International Journal of Eating Disorders* 21(4):367–376.

Pope, H.G., and J.I. Hudson. 1992. Is childhood sexual abuse a risk factor for bulimia nervosa? *American Journal of Psychiatry* 149(4):455–463.

Pope, H.G., K.A. Phillips, and R. Olivardia. 2000. *The Adonis Complex: The Secret Crisis of Male Body Obsession.* New York: Free Press.

Powers, P.S. 1997. Management of patients with comorbid medical conditions. In *Handbook of Treatment for Eating Disorders. 2nd ed.*, edited by D.M. Garner and P.E. Garfinkel. New York: The Guilford Press.

Rastam, M., and C. Gillberg. 1991. The family background in anorexia nervosa: A population-based study. *Journal of the American Academy of Child and Adolescent Psychiatry* 30(2):283–289.

Rhea, D.J. 1999. Eating disorder behaviors of ethnically diverse urban female adolescent athletes and non-athletes. *Journal of Adolescence* 22(3):379–388.

Rodin, J., L. Silberstein, and R. Striegel-Moore. 1984. Women and weight: A normative discontent. *Nebraska Symposium on Motivation* 32:267–307.

Rosenberg, M. 1965. *Society and the Adolescent Self Image.* Princeton: Princeton University Press.

Rucker, C.E., and T.F. Cash. 1992. Body images, body-size perceptions, and eating behaviors among African-American and white college women. *International Journal of Eating Disorders* 12(3):291–299.

Schmidt, U.A. 2002. Risk factors for eating disorders. In *Eating Disorders and Obesity: A Comprehensive Handbook. 2nd ed.*, edited by C.G Fairburn and K.D. Brownell. London: The Guilford Press.

Schmidt, U., A. Jiwany, and J. Treasure. 1993. A controlled study of alexithymia in eating disorders. *Comprehensive Psychiatry* 34(1):54–58.

Schwartz, M.F., and P. Gay. 1996. Physical and sexual abuse and neglect in eating disorder symptoms. In *Sexual Abuse and Eating Disorders,* edited by M.F. Schwartz and L. Cohn. New York: Brunner/Mazel.

Siever, M.D. 1994. Sexual orientation and gender as factors in socioculturally acquired vulnerability to body dissatisfaction and eating disorders. *Journal of Consulting and Clinical Psychology* 62:252–260.

Smolak, L. S.K. Murnen, and A.E. Ruble. 2000. Female athletes and eating problems: A meta-analysis. *International Journal of Eating Disorders* 27:371–380.

Spitzer, R.L., S. Yanouski, T. Wadden, R. Wing, M.D. Marcus, A. Stunkard, M. Devlin, J. Mitchell, D. Hasin, and R.L. Horne. 1993. Binge eating disorder: Its further validation in a multisite study. *International Journal of Eating Disorders* 13:137–153.

Steinberg, L., S.D. Lamborn, N. Darling, N.S. Mounts, and S.M. Dornbusch. 1994. Over-time changes in adjustment and competence among adolescents from authoritative, authoritarian, indulgent and neglectful families. *Child Development* 65:754–770.

Stice, E. 2002. Sociocultural influences on body image and eating disturbance. In *Eating Disorders and Obesity: A Comprehensive Handbook. 2nd ed.,* edited by C.G Fairburn and K.D. Brownell. London: The Guilford Press.

Striegel-Moore, R.H., D. Leslie, S.A. Petrill, V. Garvin, and R.A. Rosenheck. 2000. One-year use and cost of inpatient and outpatient services among female and male patients with an eating disorder: Evidence from a national database of health insurance claims. *International Journal of Eating Disorders* 27(4):381–389.

Strober, M., and C.M. Bulik. 2002. Genetic epidemiology of eating disorders. In *Eating Disorders and Obesity: A Comprehensive Handbook. 2nd ed.,* edited by C.G Fairburn and K.D. Brownell. London: The Guilford Press.

Sullivan, P.F. 2002. Course and outcome of anorexia nervosa and bulimia nervosa. In *Eating Disorders and Obesity: A Comprehensive Handbook. 2nd ed.,* edited by C.G Fairburn and K.D. Brownell. London: The Guilford Press.

Tiggeman, M., and A.S. Pickering. 1996. Role of television in adolescent women's body dissatisfaction and drive for thinness. *International Journal of Eating Disorders* 20(2):199–203.

Tober, G. Motivational interviewing with young people. In *Motivational Interviewing: Preparing People to Change Addictive Behavior*, edited by W.R. Miller and S. Rollnick. New York: The Guilford Press.

Tripp, M.M., and T.A. Petrie. 2001. Sexual abuse and eating disorders: A test of a conceptual model. *Sex Roles* 44:17–32.

U.S. Department of Agriculture. 1996. *Food Guide Pyramid Booklet*. Retrieved from the World Wide Web: www.usda.gov.

Van der Ster Wallin, G., C. Norring, and S. Holmgren. 1994. Binge eating versus nonpurged eating in bulimics: Is there a carbohydrate craving after all? *Acta Psychiatrica Scandinavica* 89(6):376–381.

Vandereycken, W. 2002. Families of patients with eating disorders. In *Eating Disorders and Obesity: A Comprehensive Handbook*, edited by C.G. Fairburn and K.D. Brownell. New York: The Guilford Press.

Vanderlinden, J., and W. Vandereycken. 1996. Is sexual abuse a risk factor for developing an eating disorder? In *Sexual Abuse and Eating Disorders*, edited by M.F. Schwartz and L. Cohn. New York: Bruner/Mazel Publishers.

Vitousek, K.B. 2002. Cognitive-behavioral therapy for anorexia nervosa. In *Eating Disorders and Obesity: A Comprehensive Handbook*, edited by C.G. Fairburn and K.D. Brownell. New York: The Guilford Press.

Walsh, T. 2002. Pharmacological treatments for anorexia nervosa and bulimia nervosa. In *Eating Disorders and Obesity: A Comprehensive Handbook*, edited by C.G. Fairburn and K.D. Brownell. New York: The Guilford Press.

Wilfley, D.E. 2002. Psychological treatment of binge eating disorder. In *Eating Disorders and Obesity: A Comprehensive Handbook. 2nd ed.*, edited by C.G. Fairburn and K.D. Brownell. New York: The Guilford Press.

Wilfley, D.E., R. Robinson Welch, R.I. Stein, E. Borman Spurrell, L.R. Cohen, B.E. Saelens, J.Zoler Douchis, M.A. Frank, C.V. Wiseman, and G.M. Matt. 2002. A randomized comparison of group cognitive-behavioral therapy and group interpersonal psychotherapy for the treatment of overweight individuals with binge eating disorder. *Archives of General Psychiatry* 59(8):713–721.

Williamson, I., and P. Hartley. 1998. British research into the increased vulnerabiliy of young gay men to eating disturbances and body dissatisfaction. *European Eating Disorders Review* 6(3):160–170.

Wilson, G.T., C.G. Fairburn, and W.S. Agras. 1997. Cognitive-behavioral therapy for bulimia nervosa. In *Handbook of Treatment for Eating*

Disorders, edited by D.M. Garner and P.E. Garfinkel. New York: The Guilford Press.

Wiseman, C.V., J.J. Gray, J.E. Mosimann, and A.H. Ahrens. 1992. Cultural expectations of thinness in women: An update. *International Journal of Eating Disorders* 11(1):85–89.

Wiseman, C.V., S.R. Sunday, F. Klapper, W.A. Harris, and K.A. Halmi. 2001. Changing patterns of hospitalization in eating disorder patients. *International Journal of Eating Disorders* 30:69–74.

Wonderlich, S., R. Crosby, J. Mitchell, K. Thompson, J. Redlin, G. Demuth, and J. Smyth. 2001. Pathways mediating sexual abuse and eating disturbance in children. *International Journal of Eating Disorders* 29:270–279.

Yates, W.R. 1999. Medical problems of athletes with an eating disorder. In *Eating Disorders: A Guide to Medical Care and Complications*, edited by P.S. Mehler and A.E. Andersen. Baltimore: Johns Hopkins University Press.

Zeman, J., and J. Garber. 1996. Display rules for anger, sadness, and pain: It depends on who is watching. *Child Development* 67:957–973.

Bethany Teachman, Ph.D., is assistant professor at the University of Virginia in the Department of Psychology. She received her Ph.D. from Yale University. Her research focuses on cognitive processing that contributes to psychopathology, and her clinical background includes serving as assistant director of the Yale Psychological Services Clinic, and working as a therapist at the Yale Center for Eating and Weight Disorders and at Massachusetts General Hospital. She is currently a therapist at the Ainsworth Psychological Clinic in Charlottesville, Virginia. Teachman is also an author of Treatment Planning in Psychotherapy: Taking the Guesswork Out of Clinical Care.

Marlene B. Schwartz, Ph.D., is codirector of the Yale Center for Eating and Weight Disorders. She is also associate research scientist and lecturer in the Psychology Department at Yale University, where she teaches graduate courses and supervises student research and clinical training. She received her Ph.D. from Yale University. Her current research focuses on the role of society and family in the prevention and treatment of eating disorders and obesity.

Bonnie Gordic is a research assistant at the Yale Center for Eating and Weight Disorders and the Yale Center for Child Development and Social Policy. She received her B.A. in Psychology from Yale University. Her research interests focus on the families of children with eating disorders and on early childhood intervention and social policy.

Brenda Coyle, Ph.D., is clinical director of the Yale Center for Eating and Weight Disorders. She received her Ph.D. from Boston College and completed postdoctoral fellowships at Harvard Medical School and Yale University. Her primary clinical interests involve the prevention and treatment of eating disorders and obesity. In addition to teaching graduate students and directing the clinical services at Yale, Coyle is also a licensed psychologist in private practice specializing in women's health.

Foreword author **Kelly D. Brownell, Ph.D.,** is professor of Psychology, Epidemiology, and Public Health, director of Graduate Studies, and director of the Yale Center for Eating and Weight Disorders at Yale University. He has served as president of the Society of Behavioral Medicine, the Association for the Advancement of Behavior Therapy, and the Division of Health Psychology of the American Psychological Association.

Some Other
New Harbinger Titles

The Turbulent Twenties, Item 4216 $14.95

The Balanced Mom, Item 4534 $14.95

Helping Your Child Overcome Separation Anxiety & School Refusal, Item 4313 $14.95

When Your Child Is Cutting, Item 4375 $15.95

Helping Your Child with Selective Mutism, Item 416X $14.95

Sun Protection for Life, Item 4194 $11.95

Helping Your Child with Autism Spectrum Disorder, Item 3848 $17.95

Teach Me to Say It Right, Item 4038 $13.95

Grieving Mindfully, Item 4011 $14.95

The Courage to Trust, Item 3805 $14.95

The Gift of ADHD, Item 3899 $14.95

The Power of Two Workbook, Item 3341 $19.95

Adult Children of Divorce, Item 3368 $14.95

Fifty Great Tips, Tricks, and Techniques to Connect with Your Teen, Item 3597 $10.95

Helping Your Child with OCD, Item 3325 $19.95

Helping Your Depressed Child, Item 3228 $14.95

The Couples's Guide to Love and Money, Item 3112 $18.95

50 Wonderful Ways to be a Single-Parent Family, Item 3082 $12.95

Caring for Your Grieving Child, Item 3066 $14.95

Helping Your Child Overcome an Eating Disorder, Item 3104 $16.95

Helping Your Angry Child, Item 3120 $19.95

The Stepparent's Survival Guide, Item 3058 $17.95

Drugs and Your Kid, Item 3015 $15.95

The Daughter-In-Law's Survival Guide, Item 2817 $12.95

Whose Life Is It Anyway?, Item 2892 $14.95

It Happened to Me, Item 2795 $21.95

Act it Out, Item 2906 $19.95

Parenting Your Older Adopted Child, Item 2841 $16.95

Call **toll free, 1-800-748-6273,** or log on to our online bookstore at **www.newharbinger.com** to order. Have your Visa or Mastercard number ready. Or send a check for the titles you want to New Harbinger Publications, Inc., 5674 Shattuck Ave., Oakland, CA 94609. Include $4.50 for the first book and 75¢ for each additional book, to cover shipping and handling. (California residents please include appropriate sales tax.) Allow two to five weeks for delivery.

Prices subject to change without notice.

Printed in the United States
96458LV00002B/613-654/A